My Black Book

My Black Book

Nicholas Charles Adams

iUniverse, Inc.
New York Lincoln Shanghai

My Black Book

iUniverse, Inc.

For information address:
iUniverse, Inc.
2021 Pine Lake Road, Suite 100
Lincoln, NE 68512
www.iuniverse.com

ISBN: 0-595-30781-7

Contents

BOOK TWO, 2002–03

INTRODUCTION

Although most of what has been written about contemporary gay sexual relationships has been written by white gay men, most of what has been written about male-male black-white sexual relationships has been written by black men. Both fictional and nonfictional portrayals of white-nonwhite (not just black-white) homosexual relationships are mostly from nonwhite perspectives.[1]

Gay black writers of fiction who write about gay black-white relationships rather often kill off the white lovers.[2] White gay men sometimes behave badly to nonwhite male sexual partners, but are punished no matter how they behave. They may be desired, but they are rarely celebrated.[3]

---

1.   In *American Gay,* Stephen Murray wrote,

> A lack of literary portraits of gay African-Americans parallels the dearth of social science work. Other than some mysteries by Joseph Hansen, Richard Hall's (1975) mystery, *The Butterscotch Prince* and stories (notably "The language animal"), Merle Miller's (1972) *What Happened,* [along with one character, Belize in] Tony Kushner's multiple-award-winning *Angels in America,* African Americans don't exist in the gay literature except for that written by black men: 'Look at mainstream post-Stonewall gay fiction—the work of White, Ferro, Holleran, Pintauro, Virga, Aldyne [and, Murray added, Chabon, Chin, Cunningham, Feinberg, Fox, House, Indiana, Keenan, Kramer, Leavitt, Leddick McCauley, Maupin, Monette, Nava, Picano, Rechy, Tapon, Torchia, Wong, and Yates]—and you'll find it's as segregated as any "Christian academy" in Hattiesburg or Tuscaloosa' (Jurrist 1987:34). Outside the mainstream is Coleman Dowell's (1983) *White on Black on White,* dealing with a male and female who are sexually obsessed with black men. From inside the Violet Quill circle, there is Michael Grumley's (1991) posthumously published *Life Drawing.* The main two characters in the major British novel about the "clone" era, Alan Hollinghurst's (1988) *The Swimming Pool Library,* prefer blacks (the elder says all his real friends were black; the younger, who says he has no friends, objectifies his sex partners regardless of color). Gay African-American writing also has a quite limited palette—that is, it is not notable for including Latin-, or Native-, or Asian-Americans—while often objectifying blond as the only other recognized kind." The only social science study of gay black-white relationships, a survey of members of what was then Black and White Men Together, was done by African American sociologist Paul Lockman and published in 1984. (Murray, p. 237)

I consider these writings—and those of other gay male black writing (see the bibliography)—very interesting, not just as representations of black-white male relationships or as gay black conceptions of what is going on in black-white male sexual relationships.

By adding my own perspective, I do not seek to undermine theirs. My aim is to supplement rather than to supplant. Moreover, I am writing about shorter-term relationships than in those works. Some of the relationships about which I write herein were as brief as the park servicing of eroticized white phalluses recorded by Gary Fisher in *Gary in My Pocket* (1996)[4] or by Chicano novelist John Rechy (in a sequence of books beginning with *City of Night* in 1961). Others are longer, but not long-term primary relationships.

For me, as for other writers such as Renaud Camus (*Tricks*) and the various military personnel who have told their sexploits to Steven Zeeland in a series of books, what and how men connect sexually shows something important about who we are. Not that everyone passing across these pages has a gay identity as I do, but desires **are** patterned. These patterns have many buried/unconscious roots, and are sometimes broken away from. Although some people zealously follow the same script in every sexual encounter, others engage in more improvisatory theater—or are more willing to try out a role in someone else's sexual script(s).

I do not consider myself a spokesman for white men who have sex with black men. And I have no particular interest in providing "balance" to the black gay male writing about interracial sex with an account of one gay white man's experience.

---

2.   E.g., Melvin Dixon's *Vanishing Rooms* (1992), Larry Duplechan's Johnny Ray series, Randall Kenan's *Let the Dead Bury Their Dead* (1992, pp.49-72).

3.   Kenan's "The foundations of the earth" is unusual in that the plot kills off the black partner in a long-term black-white male couple. One might interpret as precedent James Baldwin's killing off Rufus in *Another Country* and the darker Giovanni rather than David in the all-white *Giovanni's Room*. And it is a friend rather than the white lover whom Darrieck Scott kills off in his dazzlingly multifaceted novel *Traitor to the Race* (1996).

4.   I find the extent of fetishization and masochism that Fisher recorded troubling. He was not timid about recording material he knew would horrify many, although his attempts to publish it seem to have been so desultory as to evidence deep ambivalence about making public such revelations.

I consider that how we connect and how we fail to connect is interesting and worth trying to understand. In this book I write about what I observed about myself in sexual congress with a series of black male sexual partners. There is evidence in what they said (or cried out!) of what they sought, what they liked, and some of what they didn't like in our encounters. Insofar as I was observing myself, I more explicitly questioned what I was doing and what I wanted. Put into the language of epidemiology, the risk factor propelling me was wanting love.[5] It is, I think, also the reason that writers write. Writing what will repel and scandalize many is an odd way to seek love, I know. But people, including writers, want to be loved for who they are (that is, who they believe they are), not for their skills at dissimulation.

To the best of my ability, I have recounted what happened. All narrators are to some extent unreliable, if, for no other reason, because they must remove from the flow and infinitely complex context of what occurred a few impressions and inevitably shape what they narrate by omitting details as well as by including and ordering them. Although I have attempted to avoid self-justification and prettying up the record to make me appear to be a better person (more deserving of love), I am sure that there are self-defeating patterns in my description of a series of sexual relationships that I do not recognize. At least behind a pseudonym, I am willing to risk exposing them (and exposing myself). I welcome counsel from readers who see both the patterns and what I should have done (and should do) more clearly.[6]

Mechanics

Like Randy Shilts' account of events in San Francisco (and Bethesda, Maryland) a few years later than those related here in Book I, this book includes a lot of dialogue that was not tape-recorded. Unlike that in *And the Band Played On...*, the dialogue here was reconstructed from memory, not imagined. Moreover, much of the dialogue included here was reconstructed within hours by one of the speakers (in my journal), not years later by someone who had not been present. The encounters and the sexual behavior reported are direct reportage, so this book might be considered a "non-fiction novel." I cannot vouch for the accuracy of the

---

5.   This is the poignant title of Benny Henriksson's study of showing trust and seeking love as the primary motivation for Swedish men to engage in unprotected anal intercourse.

6.   Such counsel should be directed to me at surya_varman@yahoo.com.

pasts some of my African American sexual partners described to me, but what I have written is how and what they spoke of their histories and desires to me.

By focusing here on my sexual relations with African American men in the years 1979–81 and 2002–03, I have not aimed to portray my life during those years in the round. I mostly leave out my other relationships, sexual and not, with those of European, Latin American, Asian, and Pacific Islander ancestries. As in most gay fiction, there is hardly mention of—let alone focus on—work (which for me was writing and being a temporary office worker). Black men did not obsess me; I did not even particularly prefer them. I have only attempted to describe what the black subset of my sexual liaisons was like: what happened, what excited me, what turned me off, how the liaisons began, and how they ended. This tells something about how some black men related to one white male sexual partner.

Although I "topped" some and was "topped" by others, I would not assume that combining the encounters and factoring me out represents how black "tops" took black "bottoms" then (or now). My whiteness was eroticized by some "bottoms" and by some "tops," and may have fit into scenarios of dominance and submission of which I was not aware for some others.

As for spoken Black English, I have tried to capture some of the switching by speakers between standard English and African American vernacular. With boldface and repetition of particularly stretched-out vowels, I have indicated special stresses (not just in African Americans' speech). Trying to record how some of these men used language in seduction was a major reason for writing "My Black Book" rather than, say, "My Latino Book," "My Filipino Book,: or "My Japanese Book," or some other collection of accounts of some kind of man whose bodies and desires I sampled. I value the creativity of "sweet talking" in its African American development; my orthographic choices attempt to render it in ways that are readable while providing at least some indication of cadences.

Prelude (2003)

I just assume that anyone I haven't run into since the time before AIDS is dead. Gay San Franciscans like me think of our small city as the center of the universe—at least of the gay universe. It's hard to conceive that anyone leaves it—voluntarily and alive, I mean. (Yeah, yeah, rationally, I know people who have moved away, though I believe it can only be temporary abandonment of me and retreat from the center of the world…) We also know we are the most ravaged center of gay male AIDS. The number of San Francisco men mowed down by HIV passed the total number of casualties from San Francisco in all US wars combined early in the 1990s. Ninety-five percent of them have been gay. So no one (no one gay, that is) asks, "Whatever happened to so-and-so?" The answer has often—way too often—been "He died of AIDS." We are too numb from watching friends and lovers sicken and die to ask about others.

AIDS casualties among black gay men have been particularly high (and are still increasing in frequency). If I'd let myself think about it, I'd have assumed that Chaz and Chuck were among the casualties. I might have infected them; they might have infected me…However, one Saturday recently, I learned that both are alive and well. Chuck called me (from LA, where he's lived the last 5+ years) and I met Chaz at a friend's birthday party. The double dose of unexpected good news set me remembering and trying to understand my own particular black history—a history redolent of jism and differing expectations about whether relations might lead to or metamorphose into relationships.

Although I do not purport fully to understand what my own desires are, let alone where they came from, I have some sense of how **I** felt. In contrast, I have only what my sexual partners said and did from which to draw inferences about how they felt. As you will see, many verbalized desires often, though subsequent behavior sometimes contradicted these statements, especially the sweetest, tenderest parts of the "sweet talk." The disjunction between lines used in seduction and what happened after the lines succeeded in "getting over" may be what is most interesting in this memoir. Not that I want to tell you how to read it or anything. I know that what puzzles me may be crystal clear to others and perhaps you can 'splain to me what was really going down?

A Tame and Distant Civil Rights Fight (1966–1967)

Before I try to recount and try (again) to understand my relations long ago with Chaz and Chuck and some of my other black male sexual partners, I'll go back much earlier. Surprisingly, I can remember being a virgin. "Young, dumb, and full of cum," I most decidedly was.

Was I attracted to black men then? Yes, in that anything that moved made me hotter. No, in that I did not recognize anything as specific as an "attraction" to black males. I honestly did not know that two males could have sex. And there were no blacks within 40 miles of where I grew up in the wilds of Michigan's Upper Peninsula.

The black civil rights movement inspired me. The Southern white opposition—the fire hoses, the attack dogs, the firebombs, the murders, and the white mobs opposing desegregation snarling and spitting—horrified me. My support was, however, quite abstract. I was too young to be a Freedom Rider. I'd never been in the South, had no relatives there. My ancestors came from the Scandinavian Arctic Circle to the Upper Midwest after the abolition of slavery. I didn't feel any guilt about what my forebearers did in enslaving Africans and working them to death on Southern plantations. That people who looked like me had done what they did to fellow human beings embarrassed me, but I did not have a race consciousness. I lived in a racially homogeneous society. The only recognized differences were Irish Catholic in contrast to Protestants of Northern European descent (German, Norwegian, Swedish, Finnish, English). There were no Jews or people of Southern European descent in the whole county, let alone Asians, Pacific Islanders, or African Americans.

I didn't fully realize that our church was the German one, or that it was shouldering its bit of "white man's burden." One of our minister's sons was a medical missionary somewhere in Nigeria. Another went to the Mississippi Delta to work on literacy and voter registration programs there. They were both immersed in helping black folks, and the congregation could sit back in their pews and feel that they were doing something without having to exert themselves beyond putting some money in the collection plate. I didn't know the term "checkbook liberal" then, or that it was a little too easy to be on the side of desegregation a thousand or more miles away from any battle lines. (Also, the members of the church mostly put in cash and were not liberal…)

Instead of a black family moving into the neighborhood and bringing along baggage of southern race antagonism, it was a white family from Louisiana that did. My mother, in one of her Lady Bountiful bursts, ordered me to show Alan, who was my age, the swimming pool. We hung out together some the summer he moved to town, played tennis, and sometimes sipped lemonade on his porch. He didn't talk about the South or start on "the niggers" that summer. I didn't yet know how obsessed he was with "uppity niggers."

That fall, when we chose topics to "cover" each Thursday in "current events," he chose "civil rights." The teacher indulged me by letting me cover movies (even though they wouldn't get to the sticks where we were for months, if at all). I didn't realize this was a faggy topic, or that I was a proto-fag. Or that there was more than a little bitchy queenly hauteur in my weekly undercutting of Alan's presentations about civil rights—which, as often as possible, focused on riots in the North rather than on demonstrations in the South, or on federal legislation or enforcement.

He had the disadvantages of being new and "foreign" as well as being less verbally adept than I. Unquestionably, I was on the right side, but I now realize that Alan was not a worthy opponent. I was passionate in my convictions, though not as deranged by them as he was by his. I also had other advantages: superior debating skills, no denigrated Southern accent, long years of familiarity with my classmates, and the moral high ground. Plus, no one else in class other than Alan had any negative experiences with Negroes on which to draw.

After months and months of my baiting and the class laughing at my showing up his ignorance, he finally could not take any more. At noon lunch, he came up to me and punched me. It was the first time anyone called me "nigger lover."

I blocked a second punch and laughed at him. "When you get fucked up by some nigger, you'll see that I was right," he snarled. He stalked off and, before the next week, changed his current events topics. He never spoke to me again. (His family moved away after that school year.)

This was the only fight I fought during high school. And it was hardly a "fight": It was less that I fought him than that I defended myself from being pummeled by someone frustrated at his inability to prevail in verbal battle. Very cheaply (I admit), it made me feel that I was one of the Northern whites who had been physically attacked by Southern whites for supporting black civil rights.

Probably "black civil rights" was as abstract for a number of those (older than I was) who actually went south to join that crusade.

College Daze (1973–1974)

It seems to follow obviously that when I got to college I supported the black candidate to represent our dorm floor: not just because he was black but because he was articulate. What he was most articulate about was mobilizing white guilt for his personal advantage. He was too busy schtupping his scrawny, red-haired girlfriend, who, some of my friends (never me, of course) said, walked as if she had an inflated basketball between her legs—not just an inflated part of a basketball player that was often up there. After being elected our leader, Lionel rarely deigned to talk to anyone on the floor, including the other two blacks (one of whom had not voted for him, I recall).

There were few blacks in my classes. My best friend was Chicano. (He was straight, but I didn't know yet that I wasn't, or even that there was an alternative.) My mother asked me if I had any friends who weren't Jewish. The answer was a few, even one very white Baptist. The one who seduced me was nominally Catholic, of French, Czech, German, and Polish background. My girlfriend was also nominally Catholic and in flight from a totally Polish background in Hamtramak. Combined, what the three of us knew about sex wouldn't have filled a thimble. The fumbling sex I had—with each of them at separate times—was not very good. Stan excited me more than Helen did, and Stan and I became lovers. By the summer between my junior and senior year, it occurred to me that loving a man and having sex two or three times a week with a man **might** indicate that I was "gay."

As soon as this idea occurred to me, I started coming out. Only some of my friends believed it. Strangers thought Stan and I were brothers. I was the older one. I liked to think that this was because I was more decisive, but really it was because he was much prettier. (By the calendar, I was six months older than Stan.)

My one close black friend, Penny, believed it. At least I thought she did. In the spring term of my senior year, she asked Stan if she could have sex with me. That is, if I was also willing, but she asked him first. I'm sure he didn't know what to say. And I'm sure that he wanted me to be the one to refuse. But he gave her permission, and I then also agreed.

We undressed awkwardly and I warned her again not to expect much, meaning both my limited stamina/control and my primary orientation being toward penised human beings. I was very easily aroused and shot off very quickly, so I had developed a routine of jacking off before I was going to have sex with Stan. I did the same before going to Penny's. I also stimulated her manually for as long as she'd let me, before she squatted on me and my tender shoot disappeared inside her. I was happy to be passive and to let her fuck herself on me, though I rocked some to accompany her rolling, and my hands were busy with the ripe black fruit of her pendulous breasts. She was a big girl, tall and filled out. Womanish, not at all boyish.

She got off noisily and I followed quietly. She said "That was super," whether from politeness or because her own inexperience exceeded mine. A while later we did it in missionary position, and I think that she faked an orgasm to bolster my ego. (If she had faked the first one, she did it with much more conviction.)

Probably both Stan and Penny expected that this "success" with a woman had made me straight, or confirmed that I was "really" straight, though neither one ever put such an expectation into words to me. Stan was somewhat reassured that I wanted to 69 when I got back that night, but continued to speculate about whether I was "really gay" and was going to find "the right woman" and leave him. (Eventually, he left me, but that's not part of the story I'm telling here.)

On her (senior) spring break, Penny came to Berkeley, where I was in the first year of graduate school. We got it on hot and heavy every afternoon while Stan was at work. It was almost as good as the sex I had most mornings with Juan Carlos, an effeminate Chicano…

She said she was on the pill, so we didn't need condoms. A few months after her visit, she wrote to say that she had "outgrown" me. At the time, I thought this meant she had found a black man to love. Or maybe a black woman. Only later did I wonder if her purpose on her trip west was to get pregnant, **literally** to grow out. It seems enormously egotistical to suppose someone would want to have my baby desperately enough to arrange for the seed to be fertilized surreptitiously. (A quarter of a century later, we met again. I was astonished to learn that Penny had been a virgin when we first went to bed. She was equally astonished by my speculation that she would have chosen to raise a son of ours without even telling me of his existence.)

Stan dumped me that summer and I moved further from campus, close to the North Berkeley BART station. I was sharing a house with a straight man whose wife had left him, and who was seeking custody of their young son. In deference to his acrimonious custody battle, I was very discreet about being gay.

I was having an affair with Bernard, a cock-hungry Jewish graduate student who was writing a dissertation about homoeroticism in William Faulkner's ever-so-involuted (and in my view completely unreadable) *Absalom, Absalom*. He ingested a lot of my cum in his tiny studio apartment just north of campus. And there was also a campus librarian named Tom, who liked to be throat-rammed. I met Tom at a Pacific Center rap group and Bernard at a Gay Liberation Front dance. (I think that I deflowered the graduate student, who had come out before he had any sexual experience, at least before anyone had fucked him. The librarian had sworn off anal sex—which he had never liked anyway—after getting anal warts from a notoriously predatory classics professor.)

I was having sex regularly, but still felt abandoned and wounded by Stan's replacing me. I was unwilling to set myself up like that again. (So I set myself up in a semi-closeted existence? How was that healthier? I ask myself that in retrospect, but didn't see it that way at the time.)

I did not feel that anyone could be physically attracted to me. I wasn't attracted to myself, though I had sex with myself often...I felt that I had talked both Bernard and Tom into bed, not conceiving or being able to credit that I was attractive to them. I didn't know how to cruise, or, rather, my knowledge of it was abstract, based on reading John Rechy's early novels. I didn't think that I could be successful at it, though I was consciously (but not very successfully) trying to keep my gaze from dropping whenever it met another male gaze.

BOOK ONE (1978–1980)

○ ○

Character can be read through the medium of individual acts.

—*John Dewey,* **Human Nature and Conduct**

My First Trick

One moon-drenched night, I was walking home. A slender black man, taller than I am, wearing bluejeans, a black coat, and a white bill-less cap was keeping pace with me across the street, regularly looking over. I didn't overshoot my doorway because I was watching him too intently to notice I was passing my doorway, but because I wanted to make sure that he was cruising me by seeing if he would reverse directions when I did. It worked! He also turned back. The second time, I stopped in front of the door, uneasy about letting a stranger into a house filled with possessions that were not mine—and very excited that my looks had interested someone enough to follow me.

He crossed the street and smiled. "How's it going?"

"Good, good. This is where I live," I told him in a bit of a daze, glancing at the bulge in his pants.

He continued to smile. "I figured that. Would you like me to come in and warm you up?"

I hadn't felt cold, but suddenly I had goose bumps. I also had a painfully throbbing erection. I didn't want to reach down to free it. I wanted to be with this man, but worried about being turned out of the house for bringing back a stranger, a black stranger at that. I cautioned that we would have to be very quiet.

We carried our shoes up to my attic room. I sat on my bed as I undressed, watching my trick undress. He had solid mahogany thighs, eggplant balls, a thick uncut branch of ebony rising from a thicket of surprisingly soft pubic hair until it was parallel to the floor. And then there was that shit-eating grin! Framed by a somewhat wispy goatee.

"Ya like what ya see?"

"I do," I said. But it's not going to fit anywhere in me, I thought. His dick was no longer than Juan Carlos's, but was thicker.

"Ya ever take anybody home afore?"

"No," I answered honestly.

He rolled his eyes and shook his head from side to side.

"My oh my. I believe ya tellin' the truth."

As much as I wanted to be sophisticated and cosmopolitan, the possibility of not being believed annoyed me.

"Ya ever been fucked before?" he continued before I had decided on a cutting remark.

"Uh, yes, but never by anything that big."

He chuckled. "Now I'm shore youze tellin' the truth. And would ya like to try?"

"I'd like to try, but I don't know if I can take it—"

"Oh yeaaah, yuuuuuu can take it. Ya gonna relaaaax and it all goin' in ya, and then ya gonna be wantin' to keep it in ya, and ya gonna end up wantin' me ta churn my cream inta butta."

The prediction was more-or-less accurate: his entry was patient and I felt that I had been turned into butter, though he did most of the churning. (I'm pretty sure that the pun was unintentional.)

Two bursts of my own cream could not dry, because they were kept afloat by streams of my sweat. Only after I shot the second one, did he deposit his own seed in my well-tilled back-forty.

Still smiling, he got dressed, stuffing Kleenex around his dick (to wash later, like good Muslims do). I put on my amazing Technicolor-dream striped robe and walked him downstairs to the front door. He stuck his tongue down my throat much faster than he had stuck his dick up my ass, almost triggering my still completely intact gag reflex. After wiping my tonsils, he withdrew it.

"Don't be afraid to like it when it be good," he advised me.

"I liked it, but I didn't want to wake the neighbors," I explained earnestly.

He smiled. "I know you liked it and it was re—uhl goooood."

"Uh-huh," I agreed.

"You take care, now, hear?"

"Uh-huh," I promised. I didn't say "I want you to hold me and take care of me and do this to me every night."

He knew where I lived, but never returned for more.

The Watch on Strawberry Creek

I went to see at least forty old films a month at the Pacific Film Archives or at the University Theater. It was at the University Theater during a crowded Bette Davis Saturday matinee double-feature that I met Jim. Before the lights dimmed, I noticed a gym-toned black man with thick eyebrows and a thick mustache sit down in the seat on my right. As soon as "Watch on the Rhine" started, a solid leg pressed against mine. I pressed back.

I debated placing my hand on his thigh, feeling like a teenager befuddled by my date's touch on a movie date. Except that we were not on a date. We didn't know each other. We hadn't even made eye contact. We watched Bette Davis be brave and send Paul Lukas off to try to save the world from the Nazis. Being powerfully distracted, I don't know how gripping the drama on screen was.

Surely, we were not going to stay like this through the second film? I don't remember what it was. Something I had wanted to see when I went to the theater, but my seeing it had faded in importance. I read his quizzical look as an invitation when the lights came back and our legs were still firmly pressing against each other's.

Out on University, he said, "My name is Jim and I live nearby. Would you like to come over to my place for a drink or something?"

A drink and something, but neither of us pounced on the other right away. The awkward tentativeness of the theater continued.

Finally, he reached over and kissed me. I wrapped my arms around him. Soon my shirt and pants were open and his head was bobbing in my lap.

After he'd brought me off, his face returned to mine. We kissed for a while, and he put my hand in his lap. "I don't suck cock," I informed him. "If you want to fuck me, you can." He looked surprised, but decided, "OK. Let's move to the bedroom." There, we took off all our clothes. He penetrated my butt and, after finishing back there, he swallowed my wand again. This was for me the natural sequence, though I knew that he wanted me to suck his cock. It was not huge, but plenty big enough that I was sure that I would gag on it. I didn't care whether I fucked him, but I knew that he cared about not being blown.

Being a fairly complaisant gay cinéaste counted for something, though, and he asked me on an afternoon movie date for the next Saturday—to see Simone Signoret as "Madame Rosa." I was mortified to arrive late, but we got into seats before the previews ended. During the film, he put his arm around my shoulders, and I grasped his thigh. We'd made some progress!

This time we went directly to the bedroom. Jim asked me if I would lick his dick. I would, I did, but, if he thought I would be so excited by doing this that I would want to put it in my mouth, he was wrong. After he sucked me off, he suggested I sit on his dick. Then he blew me again. Then we went out for Peruvian food.

The next weekend he had a friend's car and he drove to the Russian River. After what seemed an endless trail, we came upon the "nude beach," a clearing along the river devoid of any sand. We got naked. I went in the water. He didn't. He knew people (from his gym). I didn't know anyone.

"Where do people go here to have sex?" I asked after a while.

He motioned back in the woods. "Who do you want to have sex with?"

"With you."

He laughed. "But we have sex in bed where it's comfortable. Why would you want to do it again here?"

"So you wouldn't like to fuck me in the woods?"

"What a nature boy! He swims, he frolics in the woods—"

"But he can only lie in the sun so long without burning. And he is burning for you!"

He was amused and led me into the woods.

I found a fallen tree to lean on, and did myself while Jim stuffed my chute with his meat.

"Satisfied?" he asked after we'd both unloaded.

"Very," I purred.

"You like sex a lot, don't you?" he mused.

Although it sounded more like an observation to himself than a question to me, I answered nonetheless: "Yeah. Is something wrong with that?"

"No. Not at all. I just can't figure out such a wild gay boy as you who don't suck no cock."

"I get bored quickly doing it, and choke, or I choke right away. It does no one any good for me to try."

"But you like to get sucked off."

"Yeah. I do, but I put out, you know: whenever you want, as often as you want."

"I know. I wasn't complaining, only trying to understand. You could get over gagging. The gag reflex can be desensitized—"

"But I'd still be bored after a minute, or less. There's nothing about taking a cock in my mouth that I like. Feeling it grow, maybe, but then it's 'What am I doing with this?' It's not like I've never tried—"

"Maybe blowing me would be different."

"Yeah. It's bigger and I'd choke quicker!"

He scowled for a moment, then asked, "Are you sure?"

"I'm sure, but if you want me to show you next week, I will."

He did. And I did, with results that did not surprise me. He was vexed. I was indifferent. He did us both at the same time. If that was supposed to persuade me that I was missing something, it failed. In contrast, I put no pressure on him to let me fuck him.

Though I found our sexual status quo satisfying and equitable, our film plus sex relationship faded away from weekly to occasionally to not at all. Whenever I saw him thereafter, he was completely cordial, and once after we'd stopped dating when we both showed up alone at "Life of Oharu" (**not** a good date film) we even sat together and squeezed thighs. He didn't invite me home with him, and I didn't make any sexual proposal.

At least I knew what our incompatibility was in this case: that he didn't like to get fucked didn't faze me (I never even asked why he didn't like it), but that I didn't want to suck cock fazed him—to the extent that he wrote me off.

Shahid

I don't remember most of the men who sucked my dick during those years of disco and sexual plenitude. There were hundreds and hundreds of them, a few score of them black. One I remember fondly was on my dick in the tightest space: a video booth in the back of the Locker Room Bookstore (Polk Street, San Francisco). I took in even less of the fuck film that was unrolling than I had of "Watch on the Rhine." A head bobbing on one's dick is more distracting than thighs pressing together, you know? Irrelevantly, I noticed that his ears were very small.

"You cum good," he said when his mouth was no longer full. "I'd like ta taste you again!"

Ever eager to oblige, I responded: "It can be arranged." Before I could put my dick away, he went down for another lick that made me gasp and shiver. In some discomfort, I told him, "The batteries need some time to recharge."

"You like ta dance?"

"Sometimes."

At Oil-Can Harry's his hands were all over me. I was as much squirmin' from his touch as movin' to the music.

"For a white boy, you moves pretty good," he decided. Faint praise, I'm sure. Before I could formulate a snappy response, he continued: "But you cum even better. Ya have another load for me now?"

"Yeah, but not here."

"I have a place we can go."

I was startled to learn that his name was Shahid .(Was he Muslim? or a voyeur with a sense of humor?) Shahid was visiting from Sacramento. When we got to his friends' apartment, he left me in the living room for some time while he negotiated taking over a bedroom. I couldn't hear the negotiations, but Shahid was successful in them.

After kissing me all over, Shahid greased himself and squatted on my cock. No one before had ever done this facing away from me. I don't think that it was so that I wouldn't see his cock, which was as long as mine and a bit thinner. He spilled his seed on my shins and feet rather than my belly. My own eruption was contained somewhere up his love canal.

I asked if he wanted me to stay. He cuddled against me, and reassured me, "It's all arranged. And then we can go to brunch in the morning with my friends. And then we can drop you off in Berkeley on our way home tomorrow." ("Home" was Sacramento.)

In the morning, after he put all the pillows under his midsection and asked me to give it to him again, his Sacramento friend (not lover) called Juice, and their/our San Francisco hosts, Bobby and Ike, took us along to another friend's house in Diamond Heights. We had a festive brunch on the patio. Shahid smiled at various not-very-salacious compliments for his catch. When the host, Paul, asked where we met, we simultaneously said "Oil-Can Harry's" and looked laughingly at each other.

Juice asked how the music was. Shahid laughed, "Was there music?" and gave me an innocent look.

"Music and strobe lights, but we didn't much notice," I replied.

"Uh-huh," Paul intoned. "And a tongue down your throat and hands all ova your dick, right?"

I laughed and agreed.

"That's our little Shahid!" Bobby said.

Shahid looked abashed, but laughed, then asked, "You ever give up your bed fuh me and anybody else before?"

Bobby laughed some more. "I neva been asted so urgin-like before."

"So dontcha be giving a bad impression of me!"

"By now, Nicky already have his own impression a you!"

"He thinks I'm fiiiiine," Shahid told him. Both turned for confirmation to me.

"Shahid, is fiiiine" I confirmed

"He throw his ass up good?" Ike asked.

"I-I-I-**kuh**! What kind of question's dat!" Shahid protested.

"I jus' knew your booty was a'sizzlin' when you came in an begged for a place ta do it las' night. An' den I heard the springs a my bed playin' a wild beat—"

"Yeah, well, that don't mean you ask someone you just met whether I'm a good fuck!"

"Ain't you?"

"Course I is, but it's not polite to ask a guest."

"I thinks a you as family."

"I **am** family. But you don't be askin' your sister if she gives head, do you?"

"Don't need to. It's hereditary." This cracked everyone up.

"Or if she be satisfyin' her man."

"I 'spects that's heredity, too. If she wasn't, he'd be coming 'round here, and I'd do the job for her."

"Yeah, well, Nicky ain't wagging his joystick in your face, so I musta given him some good lovin'—alrighty?"

It was true, but I was embarrassed, and the whole discussion had made me hard again. I hoped it wasn't obvious, but Paul said, "You're welcome to borrow my bedroom if you wanna, um, if ya wanna get away from these here oafs and have some privacy."

This made me blush even more seriously. Ike beamed, and encouraged me: "Ya got some more fo' him, and he sure be wantin' it. So, go give it ta 'im. Give it ta 'im gooood!"

Shahid nodded. "This white boy full of juice," he bragged.

Juice protested, "Don't be takin' my name in vain!"

"It ain't in vain," Shahid smiled.

"Maybe he'd like some a mine," Juice persisted.

"The two of us do just fine, OK?"

"OK."

"So, Shahid, ya gonna give him some mo' head o' ya gonna let somebody else have a taste?"

Shahid tried to glare, but giggled. "OK! Thanks, Paul. Whatever Nicky wants, Nicky gets." To me: "You want?"

I looked down (demurely?), but stood up. Everyone laughed. "You go, girl," Ike cheered one of us (Shahid, I thought).

Paul came inside with us and gave Shahid a towel. "Try to keep yore jism on this, OK?"

Shahid mocked a hurt look. "I'm not so full of cum that it's gonna overflow with one more helping."

"Well, you know, if you wanna do yourself, too."

The bedroom contained a king-size bed and a whole lot of mirrors. On every wall, and, yeah, on the ceiling too. "Paul likes to watch himself," I suggested, as I started to undress.

Shahid stopped me from taking off my shirt, after I'd unbuttoned it. "I'm not sure it's himself he watches. If you don't mind, I'd like it to be like the first time. Ya know? With your pants around your ankles."

"We have a lot more room, now," I observed. "A very **big** bed."

"Well, I like you with your pants down, bunched up around your ankles."

"And me standin' up?" I was nothing if agreeable.

"Nah. Why dontcha sit down and open up those furry legs, so's I can lick yore candy cane real good and make it shoot out some more of your sweet love juice?"

My legs had to be together to peel down my pants, and then they prevented opening my legs very wide, but I could spread my knees, and that gave him access to my balls, which he licked and popped in and out of his mouth. When he moved up to swallow the sword, he opened up his own pants and put the towel in front of him, draping it over the barrier of my pants.

"Jus' a second," I said. I raised my legs over his head and lowered my jeans-shackled feet behind his back. Now he was entirely between my legs. He adjusted the towel, swallowed the sword again, and worked both our dicks until they exploded.

For the last time, alas. I didn't go to Sacramento, and he never called me in Berkeley. I was sorry that I never got to see him shoot off; I only saw the proof after the fact.

Me and Julio, Down by the Schoolyard

I was waiting for a bus after leaving the I-Beam, a gay disco on Haight Street in San Francisco. A short young black man asked me where I'd been. Slender as he was, his ass jutted out substantially, I noticed. The long jacket he was wearing prevented gauging the front matter with any precision, but the curve in back was unmistakable even from the front. If he'd been hulkier I probably would have just said "Dancing," but I named the place, the I-Beam.

He then asked me, "Do you give good head?"

I honestly answered "No."

He continued, "It looks like ya got a hot booty, do you know how to move ya' hips around a man's thang?"

I must have been a little, umm high, because I continued to answer honestly: "Sometimes."

He hoisted his jacket above his waist, opened his fly, and took out his semi-hard scimitar (it was curved like one, though cylindrical.) Flashing his Ultrabrite smile, he asked "Would ya like me to stir your shit up with this?"

His forthrightness amused me. I wondered if he fucked as good as he talked.

We didn't have any place we could go to bed together. (I hardly ever took tricks home—but then I didn't usually bend over for men I met in the street, either, or for strangers I met anywhere!) He suggested a schoolyard somewhere between downtown Oakland and Berkeley and we got off.

I found a place behind a temporary structure where we would not be visible even from the deserted playground. I lubricated myself and called him over.

"Oh, yeaaah, that's re-e-e-uhl goood. I like that! Youze all ready. Yore man-pussy all greased and ready to be stuffed? Just bend over and get ready, 'cause what you want's right here! And I'm gonna give it ta ya re-e-e-uhl good. You gonna be beggin' me not to stop! Now ya just wiggle those hips and show me you want it up the butt. Yeah, like that. Now open the door for me to come in." I bent further over. I couldn't grab my ankles, because my hands were spreading my ass-cheeks apart as he'd ordered.

26

He plunged it in, rooted around a little, got off quickly, and hurried away. Get the goods and get away...It wasn't good enough to make me think about begging him to keep on. However, I'd have preferred him not to finish so quickly. Was it his fast-shooting that made someone, sometime beg him not to stop? I didn't. Nor did I particularly mind that he fled after he got what he wanted. Although I had never had any illusion that I was starting a relationship with this half-pint trash-talker/exhibitionist, I thought the fucking would last long enough for me to get off a load, too. Still, I was more amused by his line and my accepting it than I was disappointed by the sex itself.

I had a long walk home and then masturbated, thinking of Juan Carlos. Sex with Juan Carlos was always good, even when he was far away...

Another Tongue, Another Place

While not celibate, I had not experienced "promiscuity," that is, rapid anonymous public sex...until I entered the backroom of the Jaguar Bookstore one Saturday night. There, I made up for lost time. I doubled the number of men I'd had sex with in my whole life in one night, and I came ten times: eight times in mouths, twice in rear ends, one of them black.

The only thing I'd blown was my own mind, but that was completely blown by the scene and by how I'd thrown myself into it. I felt that many men had found me attractive. (Now, I think that it was more that a hard cock is good to find, and that there were many more men hungry for hard cocks than there were hard cocks.)

I'm sure I had a big grin on my face, as I walked up 18th Street toward Castro, where I'd parked the car that my landlord had left me for the weekend (between driving him to and from the Oakland airport). A tall black man with large but deep-set eyes under low, thick eyebrows was sitting on a stoop, gazing intently at me. He hailed me, "You look like youze havin' yaself a real good time."

I stopped and smiled up at him. "You're right."

He got up and moved down enough steps so our heads were at the same level. "You been havin' a good time by yaself?"

"No. I've had lots of company."

"I don't see none. Where's it at?"

"In the Jaguar Bookstore, or behind it."

"I see, I see! You already got your rocks off."

"Ten times," I bragged.

"My, my, my. Anyone tap that pretty butt ya got on yuh?"

I must have looked surprised, because he continued, "Nobody ever tole ya 'dat ya got a pretty butt afore?"

"Not that I recall," I answered shyly—ludicrously shyly for someone who'd had a lot of sexual action in the preceding hours.

"Nobody tasted that side tanight?"

"No."

"It ever be—uh tasted?" he asked slyly.

"Yeah. It has."

"It taste gooood?"

"I don't know."

"I wanna taste it! Will ya let me?"

"You talk this shit to everybody that goes by?"

"Nah. Nobody wit' a butt like yours been by here. An' you looks real relaxed. You don' look like someone's gonna be rude—and may be, maybe someone's who'd like to get rimmed real slow and then fucked real deep. Am I right, or what?"

"Rimmed real slow and fucked real deep," I repeated, trying out the idea, considering if that was what I wanted when I thought I was done with sex after a very busy night of it.

"Dat's right. Ta complete yore good night."

We went on to determine that in the morning I would bring him back from Berkeley to The City. He lived way out in the mildew zone, nearly in the ocean.

On the Bay Bridge, we learned that we'd overlapped at U of M for my last two years. He had been on the basketball team, had a high free-throw percentage, but had not been a star. (Not that I'd have recognized even a star's name. I never saw a Michigan basketball game.)

When we got inside, he asked me to rinse my ass. "There's no cum up there, right?" has asked again.

After I'd washed thoroughly, I wrapped a towel around my waist and went into my bedroom. Rufus was naked there, ready for inspection. I ran my eyes up and down the splendid specimen of masculinity. His waist was surprisingly small, but everything else about him was big. His feet dangled beyond the edge of the bed. His dick was long, not especially thick (though not a pencil either!). It was not hard.

I lay down beside him. He moved me to the middle (lengthwise) of the bed. Then he lifted up my ankles. My legs were parallel to my trunk, but he wanted a still solider base. I had no idea that my knees could touch down next to my head! I had never been that limber before. He knelt and kept his promise. Very soon I was quivering like a bowl of pudding in a 6.0 earthquake. (Any greater magnitude, it would crash to the floor from so precarious a position.) Almost as astonishing as the novel position was a familiar sensation. My cock was as hard as if no one had touched it all night. He knew where my on button was and flicked it to "on" with his tongue.

He took periodic sniffs at a bottle of poppers. (At the time, I didn't know what it was.) These made him more ardent—or at least more frenzied. (When was he not ardent?) What he was doing made us both shiver—

The chute was so wet, that I didn't think that I needed lubricant, but Rufus knew better than I did what I needed—and what I wanted—and how to give me what I wanted in ways I hadn't known were possible.

My knees were squeezing my ears and I had never before been as open as I was. I guess that my ass was too high in the air for Rufus to kneel to enter it. He crouched, so that what I could reach were the smooth backs of his legs below his bulging calves. I held on, not wanting to upset his balance by pulling too hard on what I could reach. I couldn't pull him deeper inside me anyway, because he was already in the full—and not inconsiderable—length of his drilling equipment. "Looks like ya like this," he said, stating the obvious.

I nodded, hoping that no play-by-play commentary was going to start.

Just a few exclamations of "Baby, oh baby!" And he skillfully extracted the eleventh load of the night with his right hand. He was not far behind. Deep **in** my behind, yes, and, in timing, just behind me.

I was somewhat surprised that I could lift my legs, but I could. I stretched them the other way, curving my frontside toward his.

Rufus was almost a foot taller, so that when my head was under his armpit and my face was pressed against his hard, but not particularly jutting chest, our limp cocks were pressed against beside each other (mine on top).

I woke up not because it was light (though it was), but because his tongue was in my spookie again. I groaned, "What are you doing up so early And up **there** so early!."

"Getting me another taste," he responded. He pushed his tongue in, pulled it out, and sarcastically asked, "It bother ya?"

"You know it bothers me—bewitched, bothered, and bewildered is what you make me!"

"He came up for more air, which he used to ask, "I kin see the first two, but what bewilders ya?"

"**How** you bewitched me."

His tongue made several quick circuits. "Like this!" he explained helpfully.

"The way you do the things you do," I murmured.

"You like the things I do?"

"I like how **you** do them. And don't pretend you don't already know that!"

"Well, good. You're gonna remember this morning as the morning Rufus took you from behind."

He did and I do—and, less memorably, I did myself onto the towel I had worn in from the bathroom a few hours earlier. The statistic twelve times in less than twelve hours impressed me, but I'd forgotten all the men involved in my coming out as an ejaculation machine except this last one.

He didn't have time for breakfast. He had to get home. He had to get home before his jealous husband got home from working the night shift. That he had a husband was not what I wanted to hear. It surprised me that he was in a relationship in which he wasn't the husband. I was much more disappointed that the reamings of this late night and early morning had not been the beginning of a beautiful relationship than I was concerned about the jealousy of someone I hadn't met, and had only just learned existed. Nonetheless, I was curious: "You rim him like you rimmed me?"

"No. He thinks he's da man."

"And he's your man?"

"Dat's what he say."

"And what do you say?"

"I say 'You da man; youze my man.'"

"And you're his woman."

"I'm nobody's woman, but he takes care a me."

"And that's why you were out on the street at 2:30 in the morning."

"He takes care of me good, but he don't give it up, and, **you** knows, I like to fuck, too."

"Yeah, and, as **you** know, I like how you fuck"

"Oh, yeah! I know. You're a great piece of ass, and I could get hooked on you, re-e-e-uhl easy."

"But you don't want to?"

"It's impossible. Ken would kill us both. And you'll move on when you finish school. I loved eatin' yore ass and fuckin' yore ass, but my future's with Ken."

"Why? Your real name 'Barbie'?"

This made him laugh. "Sometimes, I think dat **he** think it is. But usually it's good, and he makes me coo."

"And he taught you how to pry open a man?"

"Nah. I already knew that."

"But not how to get into Ken-doll."

"Nobody could get up into that man's rear end. It be locked tight."

"And he has your key?"

"Dat's right. Nobody else but him fucks me."

"But you fuck somebodys else, somebody elses—I mean, other men's."

"Yeah—as long as he don't find out."

"Well we'd better get you home so he **doesn't** find out."

"Yeah, Puh-leeeze. And don't take it hard, OK"

"That's the only way you give it."

He chuckled, "You know what I mean. I like ya. I like ya a lot, but I'm married, ya know?"

"I do now!"

Would knowing it earlier have stopped me? If it had, I'd have missed gymnastics that surprised me. I would not have learned what a tongue could do or that I could be stretched out the way that I had been. I was sorry that it was over, but not sorry I'd been "seduced." I was sorry that I was being abandoned after such goooood lovin', sorry that there weren't going to be any repeat performances.

There were more men, some of them black, and I went with some more. But soon after discovering the sleazy backroom troughs, I discovered the real pleasure palaces.

Putting on a Show

There was a large window between the video room and the maze at the old Ritch Street baths. I'd just cum and while, you could say, my seminal ducts were refilling, I was standing in front of the window between the maze and the video room, watching a fuck film. A svelte and very lithe black man, very much my type—smooth and café-au-lait colored, not super-hung but definitely endowed—came up behind me and reached under my towel to finger my dry butthole.

I had never been fucked at the baths before, and never (before or after) in front of an audience, but having seen what he looked like and made up my mind to let him "have his way with me," I turned back to facing the film, bending down some, thereby sticking my butt out at him more. He reached around my waist to unknot my towel and draped it around my neck, then lubricated me thoroughly. (I have no idea where he was carrying the lubricant!). I braced myself and swayed slightly from side to side as a growing audience watched him hump me.

There were murmurs of excitement and appreciation. Somewhat unusually, no one approached. We were performing in the light. They were in the semi-darkness, and they stayed there. Is "transfixed" the word? I was transfixed by this gorgeous man who came up and started fucking me and I thought that everyone else present shared my awe. I now doubt that that was it, but there must have been something about the lighting and the light (me) and dark (him) pairing that was so visually arresting that the audience stayed back. I found it thrilling. I still find it exciting to remember It was my brief stint as a porn star, in a live-action sex show.

After he shot his best shot, he whispered thanks in my ear. I smiled and turned around, and his lips enveloped mine. This was a surprise! I had plenty of experience with men who would give their ass or their dick to me and withhold their lips, and if there was kissing, it was foreplay, not postplay. I wondered why he didn't say anything else, but his "thanks" was more than I said. I may have beamed.

Perfect moments are a kind of moments, by definition, fleeting in duration, though preserved lifelong in memory. The only true paradises are remembered ones, right? Why does something have to be over to be remembered?

Another Perfect Moment

I have another memory of (a glimpse of) paradise that was only a few yards away and a few weeks later. This one I was able to watch myself rather than having to imagine how we looked.

There was a room at the end of the hall that was larger than the other cubicles. Stretching across the full six and a half feet was a very black, very smooth naked body. East African, or of East African descent. His long and muscled legs were parted. I could see a splash of white around the portals of his rear gate. His cock must have been smothered in the pillow that was lifting his ample ass a little bit higher still.

He watched me look at his bottom. I don't know whether my pupils dilated. I know that my cock did. I swallowed and met his gaze. It was intense. Though our eyes were locked, my peripheral vision detected two grinds into the pillow.

I stepped inside the room, closed the door, and removed my towel. He did not reach for what he was going to get as soon as I knelt over him. As I guided my missile to his well-marked target, he watched in the full-length mirror on the wall behind. I leaned back, hoping that he could see the hilt of the sword his butt had swallowed. I could look down at it, and had a better angle for seeing it in the mirror than he did. He was purring——and watching himself purr, or just watching being mounted by me.

I was watching my buttocks clench as I thrust into him. He was rolling gently under me.

I lay down on top of him. The pillow and the mounds of his ass lifted my own ass so high that I looked like a camel: a very happy camel with an undulating bifurcated hump. We were both watching the sex and watching each other watch the sex. He licked his lips at me. I licked my lips back at him. A kiss is not always just a kiss, or doesn't even have to involve lips touching lips.

I was more than ready for him to lift me. I caressed his thighs, but did not try to raise his body to where I could jack him off or he could jack himself off.

I had to close my eyes when I started to cum. His gentle rolling motion gave way to milking every drop by clenching and relaxing his sphincter.

When he completely relaxed the muscle, the limp survivor of my explosion inside him fell out. His arms remained crossed under his head. He made no move to touch me or to touch his cock. Indeed, he didn't move anything. Not even his eyeballs. His gaze remained on the black hills that I was no longer covering.

Only when I stood up did he turn his head.

Reaching for my towel, I said, "That was great." This cliché provoked a glimmer of a smile, but no words from me. I always thought of myself as being very verbal, master of quick repartée, but could think of nothing to say.

Unsure what to do, I left. I left the door slightly ajar, and heard it close as I was walking away. It pleased me that his splendiferous ass wasn't immediately back on the market.

Not that I was ready again, but after taking a shower, I walked by his room again. The door was shut and no sounds were audible. A while later, I head someone panting behind the closed door. The next time I passed, there was an old white butt thrust toward the door, as the man offering it watched whoever looked into the room in the mirror he was facing. A wadded-up towel blocked the view of his cock (not that it was of any interest to me).

Two perfect moments. Perhaps one of the viewers of the first remembers what he saw. I was half the audience for the other show, and I remember what my ass looked like as I rode him, and what his ass looked like both from the vantage point of the doorway and from the reflection of him under me in the mirror. And I think I would recognize the face that I watched watch us. But I've never seen it again.

Jeremiah

Jeremiah's backside was not as elegant as the mirror man's. His room was not as elegant either. He was as tall, but 30 or 40 pounds heavier. He was wearing white athletic knee socks with orange and red rings at the top. He had heavily muscled calves and thighs. And above them were what looked like two bowling balls.

As my eyes bulged from the hallway, he grinned, and told me, "It's for you baby, if you can ride it." I had no idea how literally he meant "ride"!

After I stepped in and closed the door, he removed my towel and licked my already-stiff dick. "Mm-hmmm. I'm going to like you." Probably he meant the part of me that he was sampling, not me as a person, but I wasn't sure.

"If I rear up, will it be OK?" he asked. I looked puzzled. I was puzzled! "I mean do you want to take me from above or from behind?" I thought I knew what this distinction meant, though I was not completely certain, and replied, "Whatever you like best."

He meant that he wanted to kneel on all-fours rather than lie down: he slid his knees forward, raising his ass in the air. I knelt behind him, and checked the lube job. It seemed thorough. I couldn't help noticing something very large dangling from the other side. It looked as big as a quart bottle, and the nozzle of foreskin also rather resembled a bottle top. By several measures, this was one big man I was preparing to fuck!

"Stick it in me, baby," he directed. "I want to feel you inside me."

If he had been fucked very often by anyone his own size, I doubted that he would be able to feel anything from being fucked by me. I felt pint-sized, but if there was a size test, I'd already passed muster, hadn't I? He'd seen it, licked it, and it seemed to have passed inspection. So I plunged in. He involuntarily jerked forward, moaned softly, and then pushed his ass back at me, wriggling around what I'd inserted. Contrary to my fears, I was not crushed between the two bowling balls nor lost bouncing off the sides of the cavern inside.

Pretty quickly, Jeremiah was bucking and neighing, and I was clutching his sides to keep from being thrown off. It was a wild ride, and a noisy one: he gave me a flood of verbal encouragement along with a quantity of moans that I could imagine anyone he fucked might emit, which is to say a very large quantity.

The walls shook; those trying to rest (or connect) in neighboring rooms must have felt that a prolonged earthquake was rocking the city or that someone was beating down the walls. Not because I was fucking him so hard. Just keeping in the saddle was all I could do. When he coaxed the first spurt of juice out, he moved more gently, and, I think, cried out louder—or, because he was bucking less, I was able to register some signals from the aural channel instead of concentrating on my balance and not having my cock break off in any of my mount's violent movements.

When he collapsed in a pool of sweat, my organ slipped out. It came to rest on top of his, which was stretched under him. And, let me tell you, all of mine rested on only a **part** of his.

After catching our breaths, Jeremiah said, "You really **can** ride."

"That was the wildest ride I've ever been on," I said, quite truthfully.

"You're going to be on more!"

"Oh?"

"I'm gonna make you want nobody but me!"

"Oh?" I repeated, more frightened than curious. "I don't think I could ever take yours."

He laughed uproariously. "No, no, **no!** Hardly nobody kin take that! Not even the 'hoes. I don't mean my thang. I mean **me.** You can do all the fuckin', don't worry about that. But you're gonna wanna be with me all night long, every night."

I was very dubious about this claim. Although exhausted by the gymnastics in a small space, I was not sure I wanted to leave the safety of the bathhouse, especially to go with someone so much bigger and physically much more powerful than myself. I did not think he was going to have one of those psychotic breaks that some men (of all colors) have when they start to think about how they liked to get fucked and here's the only one who knows how much I liked it—that whole horrorshow. Or what would be another horrorshow of being split asunder by his cock. But I hardly ever went home with strangers, and when I did it was to have sex. And to put it mildly, we'd had sex already. I was not going to be ready for more if he lived any closer than LA.

Besides, he didn't know anything about me (we had not even exchanged names yet). How could he know what I wanted other than his ass? And did I even want that again? Not now, of course, but ever again? Admittedly riding it was quite an experience, but, like his dick, far too much of a good thing—way far.

I surprised myself by agreeing to go home with him. We took 280 and ended up on a hill somewhere east of San Francisco State. He downed a nightcap (Scotch) and very soon I was asleep with my head on his chest.

In the morning he made basil-ham-cheese omelets. I was wearing one of his robes (the guest robe?). After putting the coffee mugs and plates in the sink, he asked me rather shyly if I'd like to fuck him lying down flat. I didn't think he could possible roll around as much as he had bucked the night before. I was right. He swiveled his hips some, but this time I fucked him rather than him impaling himself on what (to my amusement) he called my "joystick."

While were showering together, I took his tail in my hands (yes, it took two to handle it). He chortled, "I thought you was 'fraid of it."

"I've never seen one like it." After a long pause, I continued: "I'm curious about it—and, you're right, I'm afraid of being torn apart by it."

"You **would** be, you're right about that, but you won't be. I promise."

As we were getting dressed, he told me he'd drive me home, or, if I wanted, we could go to one of the beaches down the coast. Living in Berkeley without a car, I rarely had a chance to go to the beach, so I readily agreed.

On the drive south on the coastal highway, Jeremiah told me about his early experiences in San Francisco, living at the Embarcadero YMCA (hopping with young men like me eager to get their rocks off, he claimed) and dodging police raids of the bars during the 1960s. I did not ask how long he had been going to the baths or how often he went. I told him about my ex and my unreadiness to commit to another relationship. Now, I think that he believed me, though he did not betray any emotion, and reiterated that I was going to be addicted to fucking his sweet ass and tight hole and that I would quickly forget I'd ever had any other lover than him.

It was cold and foggy at San Gregorio (as, no doubt, everywhere else up and down the coast, and certainly at his house). I enjoyed watching the sea lions awkwardly get onto and off the rocky island near the shore. He later accused me of having wandered off, but I thought I was quite stationary.

After dinner, I wanted to watch "One flew over the cuckoo's nest" on tv. (I also did not own a television and had not seen the movie in a theater.) He told me to go ahead, but he had to iron clothes for the work week. I thought that he could have ironed them in his living room (to be with me) instead of in the kitchen. When he finished ironing, he mopped the kitchen. Maybe it was the movie. Maybe he had experience inside a psychiatric institution. More likely, he was disappointed, realizing that I really was not ready to embark on a committed relationship, however wild the sex had been. Maybe he wanted me to fuck him again. I don't know what he was thinking.

The chill inside was approximating that outside, and when the movie finished, I asked him to drive me to BART. He said he'd take me home, but I said that I lived near BART and there was no need for him to go back and forth across the bay. At least for or with me, he never did.

To this day I remain uncertain what convinced him that I was no longer Mr. Right. But, then, for that matter, how did I become Mr. Right in the first place? Did he decide I was The Answer just because I was able to stay in the saddle?

I didn't see him back at the baths, or anywhere else...But I intrigued another black man named for an Old Testament prophet there:

Jonah and the Eels

Jonah was regularly on his stomach in various rooms at Ritch Street. I thought his ass was a little spongy, but the muscle tone inside was fine. Not a dead lay, but nowhere close to giving as wild a ride as Jeremiah. (Who was? Who would want anyone to be?)

I'd plugged the open hole he offered up on two or three different occasions, and was getting ready to return to the hunt when he spoke. "Do you know that you've had me before?"

"Yes——more than once. I like it back there." I wanted to reassure him that I paid some attention to what—I mean whom—I fucked. I didn't yet know his name, but I recognized not only what his backside looked like, but the expressionless face that met my gaze from the hallway.

Now he surprised me by laughing. "I do believe that!"

"And you don't?" I risked asking. If he had not wanted return engagements, he could have signaled "Don't come in," but hadn't.

"I like it. I like it just fine. You work it good every time. You just don't give any sign of recognition, that you've had me before. When I was growing up, I had to pretend not to enjoy it too much. The brothers wanted to rip off what I would have been glad to give them. They didn't want any help. You could say they helped themselves to what they wanted."

"So you have to lie still and take the medicine?" I asked.

"I like the medicine and that's how I learned to take it, you know?"

No, I didn't, but I was curious about what went on behind the affectless mask, and about who carved that mask. "Learned from?" I asked.

"The men and boys in _____ (a small town in the "Inland Empire" in southern California), 'specially the older boys in my father's church."

"You're a preacher's kid?"

"Yeah, can't you tell?"

"No."

"We get used to waiting and taking whatever we're given," he said bitterly.

"Dick?"

"**Lots** of dick. My older brothers took turns fucking me and they also shared me with their friends."

"When you were how old?"

"Twelve, thirteen, and on, until I went to college."

"They raped you?"

"Oh, no. I wanted it earlier. I'd been staring at their dicks for a long time before I tasted any. And then I couldn't get enough—"

And still can't, I thought, relieved to learn that I had not been preying on someone working out earlier abuse. To complete the picture, I asked, "Did your parents know?"

"My mama died in childbirth when I was three—And my papa? He thought I was a sissy what that throws like a girl. He used my voice in church, but he didn't fill my pipes at home, if that's what you mean." I nodded, and he continued, "He figured I could be equipment manager for the baseball team. It didn't dawn on him that I would be sucking 'em all off!"

"Come on! Every one?"

"I did! Yes!"

"In batting order?"

"No. Not that I recall."

"You'd recall," I opined.

"And the others watched."

"So, did those you'd done stick around and watch their teammates?"

"Oh, yeah. They **loved** watching each other's cocks going in me and their friends getting done. Some of them loved the watchin' more than being done theirselves. They could see their friends' dicks hard and not have to figure out what to do with it. No one left after his turn. They **all** wanted to watch everybody else get done.

"None wanted to compete with you? Do what you were doing?"

"I don't think any of them **could** have done what I was doing, I mean service a whole team. I don't rightly know if any **wanted** to. There probably wasn't anyone else in the school that was ready to suck a dozen cocks one after the other. You know, some—er—wanted a second at-bat. Someone might have wanted to try one, but what if he didn't like it and had ten or eleven more to do? No. It was like my monopoly. I was happy, my team was happy."

"Did they win often on the field?"

"I didn't notice. I didn't care. Maybe they did, but I think they cared more about getting off than winning."

"Maybe, but I bet they liked winning, too."

"For sure they liked what I was doing, that I was doin' 'em all. Shootin' and watchin' each other get done—"

"Did you get off on their watching?"

"I got off later, remembering it. While I was doing them, I'd be hard, but I wouldn't jack off or anything."

"They were interested in each other's cocks, but not in yours?"

"That's what I thought. Maybe I was wrong, but I thought that I supplied the mouth and they supplied the cocks, and that was just fine with me."

"Any one you especially liked?"

"I like doin' 'em all. I liked to do the whole team, as a team, you know?"

"But when you jacked off later, was there one in particular you thought about?"

"Not really. I thought of one and then another and that I'd had them all—and that I would again—soooon."

"Hmmmm. If you had it to relive—"

"I **wish** I could! I'd be back on my knees in a flash! Every juicy cock, mine for the picking."

"Would you find out if anyone wanted to do you?"

"No. It was wonderful just the way it was. And, besides sucking them all off as a team, some came around separately to fuck my ass."

"They didn't call you names or beat you up?"

"No. They should have called me 'the cocksucker,' and maybe they called me that to each other when I wasn't around, but they were grateful, and they protected me if any of the other boys started to give me shit. I was part of the team. I knew my position—on my knees—and everyone appreciated a job well done down there."

"Did the coach know you were going down on his whole team?"

"He must have, but he chose not to let on that he knowed, like my daddy chose not to notice the choir members who had a particular interest in my company and made rear deliveries every chance they could get."

"The church choir?"

"Some of the men in the church choir, not all, not like the baseball team, but some fine specimens with long, thick dicks that they knew how to uuuuuse. The ones in the choir I went with were grown men. They didn't just have big dicks, but had experience in holding back. No matter how I tried, I couldn't make most of them cum with my mouth. I don't think anyone else could of, either. I mean, I was gooooood, but still couldn't pull it out of them. Except for one who loved to have me play his flute, they wanted to stick their bassoons in the other end, and when they got in they didn't want me jumping around under them. They didn't want me fucking myself on their big dicks, throwing my ass up at them. They wanted me to give it to me, not have me take it from them."

"And you got used to that."

"My daddy preached about hellfire, but his choir took me to heaven—often. If they wanted to do all the work, fine, I didn't need to shake it and they didn't want me to shake it. It was harder to keep quiet. I loved to have them sweating over me and onto me, but usually we were somewhere where we didn't want to be heard getting down."

"In the church?"

"Many times, but other places, and I got used to keeping quiet, keeping still."

"Always lying down?"

Jonah giggled. "I think more often bent over."

"But you didn't jack yourself off?"

"It would have been too messy most of the time. I don't need to cum. I didn't need to cum."

"Do you get hard?"

"Sometimes?"

I wanted to ask: "With me?" but contained my ego—or protected it, and instead asked, "And do you get off?"

"You mean do I shoot off?"

"Yes."

"Only when I'm alone."

"What if someone wants you to cum while he fucks you?"

"I can't———and most black men don't care whether anyone else but themselves gets off."

"I know that isn't true for all black men, and—um—you don't just have sex with black men—um, for instance, me."

"Yeah. So?"

"No one has ever wanted you to fuck them?"

"No one male."

"You fuck women?"

"Only once. It was nasty. I was made to be fucked, not to fuck."

"By your brothers—and the 'brothers'?"

"No, they noticed it, but God made me this way."

Taken aback, I stuttered, "Why?" meaning why did he think so.

"To pleasure God's male children, those who need some good lovin'."

Any? I had not assumed he was particularly discriminating about whom he took in where I'd recently been, but no standards? "You don't have any preferences?"

"Sure I do! Hairy white boys like you with thick hard dicks like yours that stay hard like yours."

I was eager to take the part of this message that made me desirable and to avoid being sure that he spread his legs for anyone, for everyone who knocked at the back door. But I was not ready altogether to abandon trying to understand the "logic" of his desires.

"If **what** you do is because it's what you did when you were young, why isn't the **who** the same?"

Not surprisingly, he did not decode the question "Why not just black dicks?" and took it more literally: "I don't live in _____ anymore."

"But if it has to be the same, the same as when you were a child, a teenager, why doesn't it have to be with black men?" There, I'd blurted it out! "Why doesn't everything have to be the same?"

"I don't know. Are you saying you want me to fuck you?"

"No."

"Are you saying I should stick to my own kind?"

"No. If I thought that, I wouldn't be here in the first place."

"Then what **are** you saying?"

"I'm not saying anything. I'm just curious why one part of the experience was—um, formative—getting fucked in silence and not moving and not cumming yourself—and another part—having black partners—is not essential, or even—Do you have black partners sometimes now?"

"Sure. What you're asking is why I have to take the same position, but now I do it with all colors?"

"Yeah, not that there's anything wrong. I'm not complaining, you know. You know that I'm a return visitor, so it's not like I'm trying to persuade you to only be available only to blacks."

"Back then, I didn't know any white boys. If I had, I'd have done them too, even though, you know, of course, there are some 'brothers' who would like a monopoly—"

"Have you ever had a lover?"

"I had a big black man who thought I was his wife, but a lover? No."

"And he turned you off black men?"

"No. It's surprising he didn't turn me off men, but I still love dick. Any flavor, any time, down my throat, up my ass, doesn't matter. Well, OK, I like getting fucked more, but I'm an equal opportunity juicer, and it looks like you're building up a new supply. Is it for me?"

"If you want it."

He laughed to himself, then told me what he was laughing at, "What comes out is always white. Doesn't matter if the thing is black or white or blue or yellow: they all love me and the cum's always white."

No doubt naively, I was surprised that when I climbed back into the saddle, everything went just like the first time. He reverted to silence and inert availability. That I knew something about him (though still not his name) and that he knew that I knew some of his sexual history and knew that I found him unresponsive—none of these had any discernible effect. I did not want to know how many cocks went where I was going on an average visit to the baths, or an average week, or an average month, or in his lifetime. I wanted to be different, not just an attachment to another hard dick, but me, Nicholas, a unique, special individual.

Perhaps I imagined him being more promiscuous than he was, because after I deposited my second load, he said that he was leaving and asked if I'd like to go home with him. He said he had a house with a view of the city lights and that he'd like me to sleep with him. I agreed. He was not sure whether I was sincere, so I suggested that, after we showered together, he get dressed and then come along with me to my locker while I got dressed (instead of getting dressed simultaneously at different spots and then rendezvousing at the exit).

His small house on the north slope of Potrero Hill had the advertised view of downtown. I went to sleep easily, which is unusual for me in unfamiliar beds, and even more so with an unfamiliar bedmate. We didn't have sex again until the sun was at its zenith. Which means that it was early afternoon when he cooked a big breakfast: piles of blueberry pancakes, rashers of bacon, half a dozen scrambled eggs, fruit salad, and coffee.

We didn't talk any more about his sexual experiences or patterns (or about mine). He talked mostly about his job, and some about his father growing up in Oklahoma. Prophetic names had been a family tradition. His father's was less obvious, Samuel, but his grandfather's name was Ezekiel, and his brothers' were Ezra and Isaiah. His brothers had wives and sons, but had not continued the preaching tradition, and Jonah had produced no sons. I did not joke that instead of being swallowed by a whale, this Jonah swallowed eels (indeed, swallowed them fore and aft...). I did ask how his father felt about Jonah not producing any sons. "I don't think he was surprised, and he pretty much ignores that I exist. He dotes on Isaiah's sons and thinks one of them will be a preacher."

"Will it happen?"

"I doubt it."

"Do you go to church?"

"Never. I offer myself on Saturday nights and sleep through Sunday mornings."

I was not going to suggest any analyses. He had stuff to do. (I had a dissertation to revise, but it did not require attention at any particular time.) He drove me across 16th Street to BART and thanked me for "a really special night."

Not so special that he gave me his phone number. The few more times I fucked him at the baths he smiled and asked "How're you doing?" instead of just returning my gaze. Afterwards, he would thank me and invite me to come again when I was in the neighborhood (meaning Ritch Street, not Potrero Hill, a residential neighborhood that no one just "happened" to be in).

In the many years since I stopped going to the baths, I have not seen Jonah. Those I've told his story of servicing the baseball team tell me that it was a fantasy—but I knew more directly about his capacity (and fixation), so I believe it probably happened. What seems to me more naive on my part was to think that he knew or could explain why he desired what he desired. I'm still trying to understand what I want and why, not least in reviewing one strand of my own sexual history here!

Get Back, Jack

He must have arrived at the Ritch Street Baths after midnight. Before seeing him, I had already been sucked off by someone in the maze, fucked someone else in the privacy of a room, and showered twice, but was still patrolling the halls in anticipation of something or another.

He was sitting up in his cubicle with his towel on. His waist was somewhat thick, his powerful legs and chest tufted. I thought his mustache quite elegant. Also, the uniform thickness of his only slightly arched eyebrows. Under them, his gaze was noncommittal. He did not look away, but also did nothing to beckon me inside. I roamed back into the maze and another anonymous mouth sucked me off.

When I wandered by again, perhaps 45 minutes after I first saw the open door of his room, it was still open. (OK, it could have been open again, instead of still.) In the interim, he had removed the towel, and was lying on his stomach. I opened my towel to show him that I was ready, and to show him exactly what was ready. He swallowed a deep breath as his gaze swept upward. Our eyes met again. When he saw my gaze move down his back, his left hand reached down and widened the valley between the two rolling hills.

That was all the invitation I required, but before I could move, his hips rocked those ample rounded hills. I stepped inside and closed the door. He smiled up at me, as I removed my towel.

Now both his hands were letting the light shine on my pathway. It was thoroughly greased, and I slipped in easily. I was glad that I had shot off several rounds earlier, else I might have cum quickly. I was very excited by the way he clenched and relaxed his sphincter's grip on the base of my cock. He was fucking himself with my cock and would willingly have done all the work. I contributed some shallow thrusts matched to his rhythm. I did not add any moans or pants. He was panting enough for two, anyway. The fourth cartridge exploded and after squeezing out every droplet of the explosive, he stopped moving. But he continued to clutch the shrinking gun inside him.

When he finally let it out, I stayed on top of him, his ass lifting mine fairly high.

"You were by earlier, wasn't you?" he asked softly.

"Yeah, but you didn't give me any encouragement then."

"I know. Everybody always wants me to give it up."

"It seemed to me that you enjoyed giving it up just now."

"Oh, I did. I **did**! But that don't mean that's the only way I like it."

Having tried to read what he'd been advertising when he first arrived, I didn't feel that I had assumed that he only liked to get stuffed. I recalled, "You didn't give me any indication of what you wanted the first time I saw you."

"I didn't?" He sounded genuinely surprised.

"No, you didn't. You thought you did?"

"I wanted you anyway I could get you." After a pause, he continued, "And my experience has been that no one is interested in my dick." Another pause, then, "But men usually want to ram their hard thingies up my butt."

"Yeah, well your behind is very fine, and when you open it, the invitation is clear and irresistible," I explained, ever so reasonably.

"Yeah? Well, I luuuuuved what you did to me."

"Yeah you seemed to enjoy it," I pointed out.

"Oh, yes, indeedy."

I waited for the continuation.

"You got some really fine legs," he murmured as he ran his hands back on down them—as far as he could reach (which was mid-hamstring). "I'd like to get between them!" I lifted both legs over his, so that his legs were between mine. He laughed. "Not like that—tho that's nice, too. But, you know, I don't have very much, but could I maybe put what I got inside a you?" He spoke very tentatively, clearly bracing for the expected refusal.

I slid off, and he turned to face me. He reached down, and aimed his weapon at me. I'd seen many that were bigger, but also even more that were smaller (even some smaller black ones). "It doesn't look small to me," I commented, quite truthfully.

"Could I put it in you?" he implored, without conviction.

"I don't usually get fucked—" (at the baths, I meant).

"That's cool. You don't have to. No problem." Three acceptances of my impenetrability fell over each other.

I ignored them: "But if you want to try—"

His eyes widened and his mouth fell open. "Oh! I'd really like to try!"

"You'll have to go in easy," I cautioned.

"Don't worry about that. We got all night!"

"You don't have to go **that** slow," I laughed.

He reached behind him for the K-Y. As he delivered the first dab, he smiled. "Nobody's been up here before me," he told me.

"Not recently." Could I have passed for a virgin? I didn't want to. I was just curious.

"But you like it sometimes?"

"Yeah, but you've gotta take your time and let it relax."

"It relax often?"

"No."

"Can I put your legs up? I know I haven't got much, but it can go deeper that way," he explained, not telling me anything I didn't already know.

He stood up, and I raised my ankles to his shoulders. "You got plenty for me," I truthfully told him.

"What I got's for **you**, every little bit, if you want it."

Would I be in this position, if I didn't? But he wanted more reassurance. "I want it, but you got to open the door slo-o-o-o-ow-ly."

He opened it slowly, but then he pounded away.

Noticing something reinflating on my belly, he laughed: "Oooooh: it be comin' back! My, oh my, we **do** like it, don't we!"

"Uh-huh," I was liking it and did not try to make any smart conversation. He started playing with my revived cock. I closed my eyes, wanting to float on the waves he made.

"You wanna come with me fuckin' yore pretty ass?"

"Yeah————Make me cum again." I managed to say.

He responded enthusiastically, "I'll make you cum 'til you cain't cum no more."

"I believe it," I sighed. But did we have to talk about it? Couldn't we just do it?

I opened my eyes and saw that his were shut. He had not forgotten about me. He was carefully calibrating his ejaculation to mine. If my eyelids were still open, my eyeballs had rolled back. I heard some of my cum splash against the wall behind me and felt more land on my chest.

"Baby, you a mess," he chuckled. "You some shooter! Do you want to take a shower?"

"I don't want to move————if that's alright."

"That's fine. Should I wipe you off?"

"Uh-uh." He used his towel, and then lay down and wrapped his limbs around me.

"You ready fo' mo'?" he teased.

"Umm, not right now," I replied drowsily. "Unless you want to fuck me again while I sleep."

"That might be enjoyable, but right now I don't have nothin' to fuck you with."

"Me, neither."

I slept for a while. I don't know whether he did. When I regained consciousness, a gentle smile whispered, "Good morning. Let's take a shower together and then I can drive you home."

"Sounds like a good idea," I agreed. "Or you could just drive me to BART."

"I have a BMW because I **like** to drive it. Where do you live?"

"Berkeley."

"No problem. I'll still have time to go home and change clothes before I got to work."

"You're going to work today? You work on the weekend?"

"Yeah. Noon to nine, today. Last night, I worked three until midnight."

"Sounds like a brutal schedule."

"Nah. 36 hours a week most weeks with two days, two nights there."

"And other weeks? More or less?"

"More, only more."

"And what do you do?"

"I'm a buyer."

"Of? For?"

"Tower Records."

"I spend too much money there."

"That's good. Means I'm doing my job."

Only then did I learn that his name was Jack and that he had lived in Glendale until moving to The City a few years earlier.

He wrote down his address (on Church, above Market Street) and asked me to meet him at 10 p.m. the next Thursday, assuring me that he would be home from work that night by ten.

A white clone answering the door surprised me. I was more surprised that Jack was going to be working until midnight and hadn't said anything to his roommate about me showing up. I didn't think he could have forgotten me so easily. The roommate called Jack at work. Jack said he would leave immediately and that I should make myself at home in his room.

Did making myself comfortable mean taking off my clothes and waiting in bed? If he'd really wanted to see me again, he would have remembered I was arriving though, and, if this was not the case, he could undress me himself.

After bursting through the door, he licked his lips, and said, "I didn't think you'd come, but I'm really glad that you did, and I'm sorry I wasn't here—and there's something else I have to tell you."

"You have a lover?"

"No, no. We're roommates and friends, not lovers. I'd love to have you fuck me again, but I have a fissure."

"A what?"

"A fissure—a tear in my ass, so it's closed for repairs. Unfortunately. I'm sorry."

"So you want me to leave?"

"No, not at all. I'll suck your cock if you want me to——and I'm ready, willing, and able to fuck you. You know that it's not that big, but—"

"You can give it a big push?"

He laughed. "That's not what I was going to say."

"What were you going to say?"

"I don't remember, but what I meant is that I want you and I can still suck and fuck, if those interest you."

"Those interest me," I said with a slight smile.

He put "I want to kiss you all over" on, and acted out the song.

He undressed me and, still dressed himself, knelt on the floor and sucked me off as I sat on the bed.

Then he politely asked, "Would you let me slide it in you again?"

"If you take it slow."

"I'll take it any way I can get it, ya know—"

He did not fuck me as hard as he had the first time, either at the beginning when he was standing at the edge of the bed, or after he lay down on top of me.

When he finished, he noticed that my cock, though pinned back under me was hard. He grabbed it and held it in that position while raising my rump. He proceeded to suck me off from behind.

When he finished, he joked, "Jeez, you really **are** full of cum, aren't you."

"I regenerate quickly," I admitted.

"You shore do. You shore do. Want anything to drink?"

"Some water would be nice."

He poured himself straight gin, giving his breath that Pinesol smell, as he told me some things about his past. "I used to look at my daddy's huge thing floating in the bathtub, and he'd tell me, 'When you get older, your thing will get big, too.' I believed him. I hoped he was telling me the truth. I wanted it to be impressive, like his—"

"—and kept yanking on it to make it longer," I continued with a straight face.

He laughed again and continued "I pulled it often, but it never got big like my daddy's. He **lied** to me. I mean, he probably thought it would, but he was wrong, and I was very disappointed. And a lot of men who think they're going to get a big black dick are disappointed. They lose interest in me when they see it, or want me to turn around. I like to fuck, but mostly I get fucked—"

"I think you fuck really hard. If your dick was any bigger, it would have torn me apart."

"Really?"

"Really. You don't have the biggest dick in San Francisco, but it's plenty big enough for me. I don't remember it getting lost when you were fucking me."

"No, it felt good."

"Yeah, it felt gooood."

Jack went on to tell me about a former high school teacher of his who kept him as a housewife for several years after graduation, liking to fuck Jack while Jack wore an apron, with nothing else under it. The teacher didn't want Jack to work, and didn't allow him to jack off while being fucked. Finally, Jack decided he didn't want to become a mad housewife or a lush, and ran away to San Francisco. As I'd already observed, he was still having difficulty with the idea that anyone would be interested in his less-than-awesome dick and, although he had rebelled and stopped playing the wife role, he still assumed he had to take the sheets every time. Not that he didn't like being taken from behind, mind you…

The first morning, I'd given Jack my address and phone number, but I only had his address. . I still entertained the suspicion that he not only hadn't expected me to show up on our date, but hadn't really wanted me to. He hadn't given me his number and he had my number, so it was up to him to call.

He was flirtatious when I saw him a few times in the Columbus and Bay store, but didn't suggest any particular time to get together. Nor did he call.

Months later, I saw him at 4th-of-July fireworks in Guerneville. He asked if I wanted to fuck him. I said that I did, but couldn't. I'd been given tetracycline for the clap, though, when the results came back the next week, they were negative. I was sorry. He was sorry. After a few more minutes of idle talk, he moved on.

Then I didn't see him for months. I sent him a Christmas card from Michigan, which also elicited no response.

When finally I did see him again, it was back at Ritch Street. Instead of his asshole or my cock, the problem this time was lack of a room. We could have gone into the maze or the orgy room, but he suggested that I take him where I found him. That was on a landing of the stairs to the roof deck. The stairs were not lacking for traffic, but we ignored it. He braced himself with one hand on the railing and lifted up the back of his towel with the other. I didn't think that I was very good at fastening my towel securely, but I must have done an exceptional job, because it did not fall off while I fucked him. Some passers-by noticed us, but no one stopped to interfere—I mean tried to join in the fun—or even stopped to watch.

Afterward, he smiled, and said, "You fuck good. You should come over some time and fuck me all night again."

It seemed that he had settled into being a bottom. I knew that he had been trained not to get off himself and to think that no one would ever want his cock. We never again discussed what he wanted, sexually or in a relationship, because I never saw him again.

My Worst Experience

As is already obvious, many of my sexual encounters (not just those with black men, by any means) were brief…and some of the brief ones were **very** intense. In some instances, I felt that I had been used and quickly dropped (like a used condom? like a soiled tissue?), but most had been physically affectionate and many had been verbally playful. Both my asshole and my cock had been fucked hard by some, but I had no experience of forced entry.

My one really bad sexual experience with a black man also occurred at the Ritch Street Baths of yore. I was sitting in my "room" (that is, a tiny cubicle) wearing a jockstrap and my black, steel-toed construction-worker boots. A balding, relatively light-skinned and paunchy black man sucked on my dick inside my jockstrap, but when I reached down to unwrap it, he fled.

I left the door open and adjusted what was in the pouch, and raised the leg farthest from the door onto the mattress, leaving the one closer to the door dangling over the side of the bed

A black man—of medium height with short-cropped hair, a thick mustache, long ears, well-defined musculature above the waist, and some more muscles stretching the unfolded towel that reached to his knees—stopped in the doorway and glared at the juncture of my legs. I didn't look away, and that was all the invitation he needed.

With the boots on, my feet were heavy, but he hoisted them as if they were weightless. Then he jammed a lubricated finger up my ass and started battering the gate with a sizable pole. I didn't think that I'd been advertising penetrability. (I know a jockstrap frames the rear end, but I was sitting down, not lying on my stomach…) And his forcible entry was hurting.

I protested, "Stop, you're hurting me."

"You honkie bitches like ta be took," he snarled.

I was stunned and was reacting slowly to the whole attack. No one had ever called me either "honkie" or "bitch" before and I was more than displeased to be called either then. I might like to "be took," but not like this! Although I was in a very poor position to protest, nonetheless I did so: "No! You're hurting me, and I want you to stop."

"I stops when **I** be done. So ya just loosen your booty and enjoy it. Ya wanted my big black dick. Now enjoy it!"

Whatever damage there was, was already done, but I did not enjoy it. I lay back feeling (and probably looking) glazed and waited for it to be over. Blessedly, this was not a very long wait. It was over and he was gone before I had time to be really frightened or angry. I could be glad that I was in a gay haven, where I could summon help. No other physical damage was going to be done. No ongoing torture or repeated rape: I was not tied up for later usage or disposal. It could have been a lot worse, I told myself. Always looking for a bright side, aren't we!

The most extended torture, a not uncommon one for those who have been raped, was asking myself, "How was I asking for it? It **must** be my fault." Given the setting, I was not provocatively dressed. I thought the boots were a butch prop. I was certainly not in a "Come fuck me" position, and he was up my ass before we made any eye contact. What did that leave to explain the incident? Being white? Or being white and gay, and therefore wanton? Or being able to afford a room? So I concluded that his resentments were general, not set off by me as a specific human being.

Perhaps I could have stopped his finger, I blamed myself. Wasn't that moment of wavering between surrender and resistance a form of "consent"? Had I been raped or just misused? Did he genuinely think I wanted it like that? Did he care what I wanted? If he thought I did, why did he think so? If he didn't care, why hadn't I blocked entry? I had to admit that I liked how he lifted my legs up. To some degree it was exciting to be taken without a "by your leave." Pain and irritation followed and quickly throttled any excitement though. Are unwilled penetration and rape different only in degree, not in kind? So, like many who have been raped, I found ways to blame myself.

(Now, in l-o-o-o-o-ng retrospect, I think the difference was substantial. I may have consented nonverbally to other men (of various colors), but at the moment where I thought I might have stopped the proceedings, my nonverbal response was my sphincter attempting to extrude his finger. So I regard it as "rape," not "miscommunication" or "unpleasant," "inconsiderate," or "too rough" sex. Unfortunately, I cannot say that I did anything to resist his lofting my feet, so I am still sharing some of the blame...)

Wild in the Streets,
Tame in the Sheets

That bad experience did not end either my bathgoing, or my black history.

I was looking at the illuminated skyline of The City from a window seat on the right side of a bus from the East Bay. I had barely noticed the brown male body beside me. Whatever reverie I was in jolted to a stop when I felt a leg pressed against mine. In the tunnel between the spans, when gravity was aisle-ward, I was certain that the pressure was intentional.

Neither of us spoke. The bus arrived in the terminal. Inside, I passed him and looked back at him. He followed me into the lavatory. Though semi-hard, I pissed. He pissed in the next urinal. "Absolutely not here," I thought, as our eyes met and our smiles reflected each other's.

Zipping up his fly, he asked, "Where you going?"

"The Ritch Street Baths," I replied. "Want to come along?"

"I'm supposed to be at a party, but I'd rather be with you," he purred.

"I live on the other side of the bay," I said.

"Me too."

"So we could get a room at the baths and be together——"

"OK. I'll say I was delayed in traffic."

Crossing under a roadway to the bridge, he motioned to a darker space behind a girder. He seized me by the waist and mashed his lips against mine. I licked the inner rim of his upper lip, and he opened my pants.

"Not here. It's only a few more blocks," I protested weakly—although another part of me was ready for his immediate ministrations.

As his head bobbed, I sighed, leaned back a bit, and closed my eyes. He seemed to have a lot of tongue and was creative in its use——and, somehow, before I even saw a mattress, I was fucking him on his knees on a mattress. It seemed to me implausibly available, to have been conjured out of nowhere for our use.

Some cars passed, but my dark clothes still covered my back. My pants were open in front, and the exposed flesh below me was dark. Nonetheless, it shocked me that I was fucking practically on the street. He didn't touch his cock, which was still in his pants, and neither did I.

After I ejaculated and our pants were pulled up, he said, "I'd really like to see you again when I have more time."

That was it? "You're not coming with me anymore?" I continued to be way behind in grasping the unfolding scenario.

"I really **have** to get to this party. But I really want to see you again. We both live on the other side of the Bay, right?"

"Right."

"So, can't we get together there?"

"I don't have much privacy," I began. (Privacy had not been a major concern so far in our relationship!)

"I have a condo of my own," he said seriously. "And a **much** bigger bed," he laughed. "Do you like steaks?"

"Sure."

"Call me tomorrow and we'll arrange some time for you to come over. I'll feed you dinner and you can feed me some more of that cock."

"You had all of it already."

"And I'd like to enjoy it again—and again—but not right now."

It was no surprise that the name on the slip with a phone number was Latino: Antonio. But my surmise was mistaken. His mother had named him Anthony, and he decided that despite speaking no Spanish he could say that he was "Hispanic," especially in Hawaii, where he grew up and came out, and where, he claimed, he had "sampled" every gay cock attached to someone under 45 and lighter than his own. He boasted that, many times, he had amazed bouncers at Hula's by repeatedly returning to the bar in a single night. He told me that he had fantasies of being gang banged, but settled for multiple encounters in a single night.

But I'm getting ahead of the story. I had another surprise when I undressed in the Ritch Street locker-room: there was fresh shit on my cock and underwear. Antonio had not really been ready to be fucked, only eager.

I washed myself and then my underwear and went on to some fleeting encounters that I do not remember.

I did call, and was fed the promised steak. It was over a thick but not particularly flavorful steak and two baked potatoes that I found out about his scarlet tropical past.

Even after shedding my clothes, I found his place overheated. I wouldn't describe Antonio himself as overheated. Insatiable, perhaps, but he wanted to just lie on his stomach and be taken again and again, and then fucked some more. After I'd fucked him six times, I told him that it was his turn to do some work.

"What do you mean?"

"I mean you fuck me this time."

"I don't really like to do that."

"Why?"

"My cock is very sensitive and it hurts." After a pause: "Don't you like to fuck me?"

"Yeah. If I didn't, I would have stopped hours ago, don't you think?"

"You can really keep cumming, can't you! You're like a one-man gang-bang."

"Well, you can keep taking it, but do you really like it?"

"Oh yes! You can't tell?"

"Not really. You don't say anything. You don't move. You don't make any noise. You don't jack off. I don't even think that you get hard."

"Sometimes."

"But you never cum?"

"No."

"You don't ever masturbate?"

"Well, uh, I have some dildoes."

"So you could fuck me with one of them—"

He laughed. "Um, I think they're too big for you—"

"And I'm not too small for you?"

"No, you're fine. You're great. I've never met anyone who could fuck me so many times in one night."

"It isn't over," I said, trying to sound menacing.

"Oh, I ho-o-o-o-ope it isn't! What can I do that will make you want to fuck me again?"

"Fuck me," I suggested.

"I really don't want to do that. Isn't there something else?"

"I guess turn over, so I can see who I'm fucking."

"You fuck with your eyes open?"

"Usually."

"But you close them when you get sucked off—"

"Sometimes."

"You want me to suck you off?"

"Not after I've been fucking you."

"You just want me to put my legs up?"

Co-operatively he turned over, raised his legs, and held the back of his knees, so that I could drive in deeper. This (or perhaps the seeming reproach of our conversation) made him moan. I watched his semi-hard uncut cock flounce about. The turtle head did not emerge from its casing.

Not well rested in the morning, he decided I was too much for a week-night. For the next several Friday nights we dated (dinner, maybe dinner and a movie, and then back to his place to fuck him 5–9 times). He told me that he had to suck off his boss on demand, and the demands came two or three times a week. And it was not a surprise that his earliest sexual experience had been with a family friend who did not want to be reminded that Antonio had more than a hole between his legs.

To provide some variety (for myself; he didn't seem to need any), I would have him sit on my cock or have him put his ankles around my neck or behind his own head. Not that I disliked entering him from behind…Au contraire…

Other than sex, we didn't have much to talk about. He had a lot of sexual experience to talk about, and various flatteries for my performance. I tended to believe the former more than the latter. He had no interest in politics or high culture or even popular culture. He had no books or magazines. No television. The few records he had were all "mood music," i.e., background for getting a dick out of a visitor's pants, getting it hard, and getting it into him. He was uninterested in playing or watching any kind of sports or in being in the Northern California outdoors, which to him was cold and colorless. Nor did he have any interest in trying any cuisine other than standard American meat and potatoes. OK, he said that he liked poi, but in my opinion that's like potatoes minus any taste or texture: blandness cubed.

Sex object to sex object we were fine. I thought that we would resume being sex buddies when I returned from Christmas vacation, but while I was home, I received a letter from him telling me that he had fallen in love and moved in with a man in Walnut Creek and was going to try to be monogamous. He said that he missed me and hoped that I would not be angry.

I was not angry. It should have been a relief to me, but, nonetheless, I felt some rejection in his settling down—or trying to settle down—with someone else. Had he found someone who could fuck him ten times or more a night? Someone who had found an interest in something other than sex that I had failed to guess? Although I could not (and can not) imagine him monogamous, I hope that he found happiness—in Walnut Creek, or somewhere else.

Moving the Other Way

Way too often, I was sitting around downtown Oakland in the middle of the night waiting for a bus to Berkeley after BART and direct busses from San Francisco to Berkeley stopped running. With Katherine, a recently divorced graduate student in another department who was also a substitute special education teacher, I found an apartment "in The City," near the Panhandle of Golden Gate Park. The black-populated Western Addition was just across Masonic Street, between us and downtown. I later realized that the apartment was relatively affordable precisely because we were serving as shock troops of gentrification.

I didn't have any sexual liaisons from the ghetto across the street. Why go out when you can get it delivered in?

Many people assumed that I was getting it in-house, first from Katherine, and—after she turned lesbian and she and her psychotic girlfriend moved out to live together—from Derek.

There was a lot of Derek. At 6-foot 4-inches and 245 pounds he had been a starting linebacker at a black college in the South. After a few years in D.C., he moved to San Francisco. He found a job in an Outer Mission district warehouse. He was living in a tiny Tenderloin "studio apartment" and had been looking for some place larger for months. He told me that places kept being rented between when he called and when he got to an apartment to look at it.

I knew that it was hard to find an apartment in San Francisco from personal experience, even for a white male-female couple, but we had never heard the "Sorry, I just rented it, and didn't know how to call you" experience.

I had had no inkling that Derek was black over the phone. He was very polite and soft-spoken, speaking entirely standard English. And then this very large, very dark-skinned man showed up and...

I asked, "Did you ever see the same listings still there later on?"

"A couple. Why? Ohhh—" He gulped. "When they saw me—"

"Yeah, I'm afraid so." Ignorance may have been more blissful than recognizing rejection and discrimination.

"And you?"

"If your past landlords and employer check out that you have income and pay your rent on time, I'm going to rent to you."

"Because you're a liberal, or because you like black men?"

"I like some black men. I think I like you. I want a gay roommate, but I'm not looking for a lover, OK? I find you attractive, but, if we had sex, things might get too complicated later."

"I hear you. We're going to be sisters and sisters don't fuck each other, right?"

"Right. I hope we're going to be friends as well as roommates, but sex might get in the way."

I did find him attractive. Since we shared a single bathroom, we agreed that either one of us could enter it while the other was in it, and from the toilet I watched him towel off after a shower or stand at the sink to shave with his big dick all but in my face many times, and from the same position he watched me towel off many times. (I didn't shave.)

I didn't like the punk rock music he played, and he didn't like much of my music either, classical, classic rock, or soul music. Our only overlap was reggae, and neither of us had very much of that.

The household functioned smoothly. Both of us liked to eat. Neither of us liked to clean. So we ate well and dust settled (except for the period while I had a Japanese boyfriend named Yoshimura who was into cleaning. For a while, every surface sparkled.) We did not comment on each other's choices of male companionship. Derek gave no indication of being bothered by how much Yoshi was around. (The two of them did not share the bathroom at the same time and were formal with each other.)

Derek complained about white men, particularly German ones he met at the Eagle, who looked longingly at him, turned around, bent over, dropped their pants, and spread their cheeks for him. He had a monumental, somewhat hairy ass of his own that he wanted to give up to someone butch enough to make him take it——I don't think this was an invitation. I wondered what I would have to stand on to reach it if he was bending over for me. I also wondered whether such logistics were part of what he considered the "problem" of men instantly bending over for him...Not that I doubted that many San Franciscans and San Francisco visitors were searching for a big dick, something he very obviously had.

He eventually found someone to top him: James, a former drag queen who had changed drags to leather—and had always liked to fuck. Had always liked to fuck men who were bigger than himself. Had never had an eager black butt offered him before. Liked to handcuff Derek so he couldn't jack off while James fucked him. Liked to look at Derek's throbbing cock while James worked a dildo in Derek's ass. But who would let Derek jack off before going to sleep, after whatever scene they'd played that night was done. Derek had found a top!

Do sisters reveal such intimate details? Could I borrow the handcuffs some night when James was going to restrain Derek by other means? (A mistake. Yoshi started wanting me to be tie him up or handcuff him every time…)

Derek didn't read my dissertation, and I didn't read (much) of the "poetry" he and James wrote. When their poetry workshop cycled through our apartment, I made sure to be gone…

So what was that about not having to go out to get it? Not Derek.

Across the Hall

Two straight boys, like me in their early twenties and on their first jobs, lived across the hall. Bob was the only other white person in the building. He worked in sporting goods at Sears nearby on Masonic and Geary. The black one, called Chaz, worked in the men's department at the Stonestown Emporium. Both had regular white girlfriends who slept over periodically. Bob and Chaz were native sons of California. They grew up together in a Monterey army enclave. Bob had been a halfback on their high-school team. Chaz had a football lineman's thick body. He was not as tall as Derek, but had big hands, big feet, a really big butt, the stereotypical black dong…I must have noticed the bulge some time in the hallway…And Chaz must have noticed me notice it.

I can't remember why the door to my apartment would have been open or ajar. From the hallway he could see me at the kitchen sink, where I was rinsing rice. I was wearing tight gym shorts and a t-shirt. Barefoot, as usual. Skimpily dressed for a typical cold, foggy San Francisco day. Radiating heat. A delectable white morsel Chaz wrongly thought was already being blacktopped by a "brother," and rightly thought liked being taken (sometimes).

When he started talking to me from the hall, I turned around and saw that he was wearing a dark blue running suit. As I continued filling and draining the pan and continued to throw back his jive, he moved closer and closer, until his cock was pressing against the crack of my ass.

He stopped talking, waiting to see my reaction. I didn't want to show any. I didn't pull away. I also didn't wiggle against him or reach back to pull him tighter against me. My own cock hardened, although my tight shorts kept it pointed at the floor. The water I was pouring off was not clear, so I refilled the pot. He took a hold of the waistband and pulled my shorts over my cock and down around my ankles. I still didn't move. He put his arms around me and pressed his cock against my crack. "I've got something for you," he murmured in my ear.

"Yeah?"

"Do you want me to give it to you?"

I thought of thanking him for asking first, or remarking that I would not have let him get this far if I didn't, but instead murmured, "I think so."

He took a nipple in each hand, twisted them a quarter-turn and said, "I'll be right back."

I thought about going to my bedroom and lubricating. Instead of laying down the welcome mat to my back door, I pulled my shorts back up, put the rice in the rice-cooker, and took out a bunch of spinach. I was rinsing it leaf by leaf when he returned.

This time he closed the door to the hall. "I thought I already had them panties down," he exclaimed.

He'd left all his clothes in his apartment, and come across the hall completely naked and semi-hard, carrying a new tube of K-Y.

"I thought you could do it again."

"Mmm-hmm. I can do it again, all right. Same place?"

"Yeah." This time I stepped out of my shorts after he pulled them down to my ankles. I continued to push the green leaves around in the water until he rolled my t-shirt up to my armpits. I raised my arms for him to finish undressing me. I stopped rinsing, but continued to stand my ground as he rubbed my ass with both hands.

"You want to do it here?" he asked, faintly incredulous.

"Why not?"

"Your roommate might come in."

Derek had another two hours on the job plus a bus ride home. "He won't," I reassured Chas. I gave a slight wriggle. That was all the encouragement he needed. He squeezed out some K-Y. First one lubricated finger, then two, then the real thing. Slowly, he worked all of it in.

I braced against the sink. I gave him a long head start of pumping my butt before beginning to stroke my own less formidable rod. My balls must have been full, because it splashed all over the cabinet doors. One spurt cleared my chin and arched into the sink, onto the spinach.

"Be sure to wash them greens good," he sarcastically instructed me.

"I always wash vegetables thoroughly," was my too-prissy response.

"I'm sure you do," Chaz laughed. "But you spilled something on your cabinets. They be a sticky mess!"

"Who made it?"

"You done it yourself." He paused. "Though Roger may have encouraged you some."

"Who's Roger?" I had no idea.

"Your new friend: the one I keep hanging between my legs."

"Ohh. So that's Roger." I'd never met anyone whose cock had a name. Was a handshake in order? "If he gets bored between your legs, tell him that he can cross the hall and get between mine."

"Thanks. I'll let him know that. He enjoyed your hospitality and thanks you for it."

Roger made himself at home on periodic visits. Usually, I received him on my bed. Whenever Chaz was horny and ascertained that I was alone and willing to entertain company he would shed his clothes in his apartment and traverse the hall uncovered. I didn't understand why he didn't want to undress or dress in my apartment, but found it exciting that a husky man was coming to my door without a stitch on and that his big cock throbbing in anticipation of my body. I wished all my deliveries arrived like that...

Generally, Chaz would suck my cock while lubricating my asshole. He didn't suck me all the way off. Like the first time, I would milk myself while he fucked me. Then, he'd go back home, giving me a view of his big black bottom on the way out.

On a rare visit to his bedroom, though, I popped the "What am I? Your woman or something?" question. Less confrontationally, I asked, "Why am I always the one who gets fucked?"

"You seem to like it."

"Yeah, sure. I enjoy it. But **every** time?"

Without further discussion, he lubricated his own love canal. He pointed to the bed, and told me to lie down there. He climbed above me and squatted on my cock, taking it all in on one quick squat. He milked me with what seemed to be experienced ass-grinding, closing his eyes while jacking himself off. Afterward, he sat at the foot of the bed, smiled, and said, "You like it like that?"

"It was great!" I exaggerated. It was good, and it put my mind to rest that Chaz knew that I was a man. At the time, I didn't think, "He's still the one on top of me" or "The cum is still cooling and drying on **my** belly." I just enjoyed my visit and the acknowledgment that I could fuck as well as be fucked. Of course, I knew that already, but I wanted to make sure that Chaz did, too.

Insofar as I was still passive, while he actively fucked himself on me, perhaps I didn't make sure enough. At the time I thought that sitting on a hard cock was more craven than taking it either from behind or on the back with legs waving to the ceiling. Sitting on it seemed to me to show that you wanted it, not just were willing to have the love medicine delivered from behind. As if getting hard and bringing myself off while being fucked suggested non-involvement! Silly as it sounds, that's the way I thought then, and I thought that the position wiped out any possible supposition that I was his "bitch" or a "punk."

Except in a three-way when he sucked me off while I sucked off a visiting friend with whom Chaz used to circle-jerk in junior high, I returned to being the one who got fucked. Another time in his bed, after I'd shot toward the ceiling, he said sarcastically, "Maybe next time I can cum too."

I was not accustomed to complaints. I wiped the splashdowns of my cream rockets, got on all-fours, and told him, "The amusement park's still open. Re-entry is permitted."

He arched his brow, and queried, "You sure?"

"Take your time. If you take long enough, I'll cum again." He did, and I did.

We continued, if less frequently for another year. In two years, we never had a date or a meal together or spent a night together. He noticed the rainbow array of men passing through the door to my apartment. Probably—but wrongly—he thought all of them fucked me, just as he thought that Derek did.

After I moved out of the building, I stopped back a few times, but he was never at home. And then his name was no longer on the buzzer.

At times, when I'm rinsing rice or washing green, leafy vegetables, I think of Chaz taking me in front of the sink and smile.

A Possible Relationship Not Followed Up

Sometimes, I wandered out to Buena Vista Park to get blow jobs, mostly from white boys. Early one Sunday morning, I received a particularly good one from a 40ish black man who seemed especially enamored of the hair on my belly and thighs.

After swallowing my load, he smiled up and said, "You cum good. You're really hot!"

"For the right man," I smiled back.

"I'd like to do you again some time."

"How about after breakfast I suggested."

"What do you mean?"

"I live nearby. I could give you some coffee to go with the cream and then some more cream."

"Yeah? I'd like that."

On the way, we exchanged names. His was Julius.

At home, I whipped up omelets, toasted some rye bread, and he told me ghoulishly funny stories about his work as a probation officer over breakfast. Then we retired to my bedroom and got naked. He wanted me to fuck his face while he jerked off on his belly (which was soft, but flat). After we showered together, neither of us suggested how we might spend the rest of the day. On the pad by my phone he wrote down his phone number and a real ghetto address: Scott and Fulton.

I thought about calling several times and cannot explain why I never did. I liked him. We had been able to talk as well as fuck. Well, we had not really fucked, but he played the flute well…I felt that he felt that I thought that he was too old, so that I'd have to take any initiative (plus I was the dominant top, right?). I didn't think that he was too old, but I didn't take the necessary initiative, and there were no return engagements.

The Man with the Silver Tongue

I was looking at a Latino-Latino fuck-magazine in Le Salon when the question "Is that real?" came from behind me. Before turning to look at the questioner, I looked over the two photographs in front of me. There was nothing out of the ordinary (for such magazines) in the positions or the good looks of those pictured, so I asked, "Is what real?" as I turned to see gleaming teeth in a broad grin, shaded by a black cowboy hat. The big, nearly round eyes above them had remained focused on my buttocks, as his view of them became a profile. After a moment, they rose to meet my questioning eyes.

"I didn't think white boys had rear ends like yours."

"Oh?" was all I could choke out in response.

He ran his left hand over the curve of my right buttock. "Christ, it is real!" he exclaimed, and turned up the candlepower of his already dazzling smile.

I wondered how it could be artificial, and managed to stutter, "Why would you think it's not real?"

I was directly facing him now, and half expected him to reach behind to squeeze the melons, or perhaps to feel the bulge in front. He raised his eyes from my crotch, and answered smoothly: "White men over 20 either have flat asses or saggy ones. I've never seen a white one as fine as yours."

"Flattery will get you anywhere; where do you want to go?" I thought to myself, but the question was too obvious to ask. I demurely responded, "I don't think it's anything special, but thanks for the compliment."

"It was no compliment. It's choice, and I'd like a piece of it."

He'd answered the question, even though I had not asked it. Somewhat primly, but smiling, I said, "It's not a piece of meat." I noticed snakeskin boots and a large belt buckle studded with turquoise and coral. Way out west drag...

Holding his smile, he continued: "No? Why don't you let me taste it?" After a significant pause, he continued, "And then I have a nice tasty piece of meat to give it." Lest I fail to understand (which was quite unlikely!) he grabbed his own crotch.

"Yeah?" I asked weakly as I searched for a reason not to accept the promised gift.

"Oh, yes," he replied with fervor. "I'd like to worship it—"

"And fill it?"

"Yeaaaaaaaah. I would like to honor it."

I rolled my eyes, and repeated, "**Honor** it?"

"Uhh, huh. It's very fine and I have something between my legs that could do it justice."

I was mentally spinning, but beginning to recover my tongue. "And you think justice is what I want?" As if you really cared what I wanted, as long as I bent over and took what was now pressed against his left thigh…

"It's so fine, I really want to do it justice."

"Mm-hmmm—jussss-tisss. You a judge? You look like a fake cowboy to me!"

"Oooooh! You know how to hurt a man!"

"Are you so fragile?"

He guffawed. "Nah. It's just a look."

"A good look," I reassured.

"But not what you're looking for?" he volunteered, trying to take the sting out of the rejection that seemed imminent to him.

"I wasn't looking for anything in particular," I said.

"What you saw in that magazine made you hard," he observed neutrally. And, rationalizing the rejection he thought was going to come: "So you a beaner and don't like 'em quite as dark as me?"

"I like how you look just fine," I answered truthfully.

"But you don't want me to worship your butt?" He sounded genuinely confused, at least a bit, probably surprised not to have succeeded immediately or been brushed off immediately.

"I'm happy that looking at my butt gives you pleasure—"

"If I could do more than **look** at it, I could give both a' us a whole lot **more** pleasure!"

"Probably, you could," I agreed.

"I could! I know that I could! Honestly, I could," he pleaded, and added an afterthought: "—if there was somewhere we could go, we could both get plenty."

"Plenty of you worshipping my butt."

"Oh yeah. I have a long tongue to get it ready, and a sweet 'ole thang to follow-through with. You **would** enjoy it."

"You're sure?"

"Most definitely, I'm sure——so can I prove it to you?"

"I certainly want justice to be done," I laughed

"I'll do it justice!"

Partly true a promise…

We took the bus to my apartment. As soon as the door closed behind us, he reached in front of me, to unbuckle my belt, and pulled my pants down around my ankles. He knelt behind me and, as promised, his tongue was long. And wide. And limber: to get in, it curled. He didn't just lick around the rim, but really fucked me with his tongue, while his hands were all over both cheeks.

—And then he opened his pants. I heard his belt buckle strike the floor. Between my moans, I managed to tell him, "My bed is only a few feet away."

He withdrew his tongue, and stood up, holding his pants at his hips with his left hand, and cupping my right buttock with his other hand. "OK, lead the way."

With my pants around my ankles, I waddled through the door of my room and toward the bed. Before I could kneel on its edge, he pushed me down with both hands. I landed uncomfortably on my gorged cock, and as my legs flew up behind me, the pants around my ankles knocked my recent "worshipper" back. His belt buckle thudded loudly, as his arms swung out to catch his balance. It bounced a bit, and landed more softly the second time. He jerked my pants and underpants over my shoes. Removal of this temporary barrier cleared the way for him to advance. He stuck two fingers as far as they could reach up my rear. "Get that ass up," he ordered and used the fingers inside to help lift it. He fluttered them inside, as I knelt at the edge of the bed with my elbows on the bed, my feet splayed, my rump up, my wet hole open, quivering with desire, or quaking with fear, or both.

Although the gate snapped shut when he removed his fingers, he pushed it open again almost immediately. I gasped or screamed or something. He kept pushing, and soon his belly started slapping against my ass. The steady humps were fast—about 75 a minute. That was less than my pulse, which was doing at least 100. I started to wiggle my bottom, but he snapped, "Don't move. I'm doing the fucking here."

I did not sigh, as I complied. Nor did my cock go limp. But when I should not have been thinking—I mean, I **had** pretty much swooned when his tongue was preparing the way of Lord Dick and again as I recovered from the first thrust of "the real thang"—the mind snapped back on. "Isn't the worshipper supposed to do what the worshipped wants?" I thought. But worshippers cajole and beseech gods to do what they want. How can I be comparing religions when I have a big black dick pounding into me, I asked myself. But I went right on: It's Allah's will that all those Muslims are supposed to bow to, when they are in this same posi-tion five times a day. "Islam" means "submission." Facing Mecca, Muslim asshole must point away from it. But Allah is everywhere, or in heaven, so he should be able to see those raised rear ends and penetrate whichever ones interest him. He's not like Zeus/Jupiter? Why would he not be interested in Ganymedes? Lots of Muslims are, and Allah supplies *houri* in paradise—probably light-skinned ones? Not that I think I have me a Black Muslim on top of me. His costume is all wrong for that, but is this man whose name I don't know in paradise at the moment? I'm certainly not, though what's bouncing down there is still stiff. It has been since I was looking at those brown boys in the magazine.

I start to run through the "Is that real?" conversation again, and start stroking the neglected *lingam*. The worshipper squats on that, right? You're not very willing to admit that you are not any longer the object of worship, if you ever were, are you? It was just a line; no one here is having a religious experience, you silly twat. There's no oracle in the pit he's digging, and it is inertia, not submission to a divine phallus that keeps your ass up and open. You probably couldn't stop him now if you wanted to. His tempo has picked up, surpassing your pulse, which has somewhat slowed. As excitement fades, muscles stretched the same way too long begin to protest.

It's going to be really messy for me to cum like this: it's going to go on the side of the bed, the floor, the sheets——If I stretched it back just a little bit, it could all go down—down on the floor. And maybe onto his boots! Oh yeah, I'd **like** to shoot some sticky goo onto those boots. His pants are bunched up around the right one, so, considerately, I aim for the left one.

"I'm not ready! Don't cum yet," he orders.

I fake a pant: "I have to!"

"Hold it back!"

"I can't, I can't, I can't, I caaaan't. Oh! I'm cumming. Uh! Uh! Ohhhhh—"

Hey, I know how to put on the Ecstasy Show.

He doesn't feel the shot in the foot. "Shit, you like it **too** much" he semi-snarls. I forget and wiggle a bit. "I told you not to wag dat tail, damn it! Mmmmmm. Daddy's coming. Daddy's got a present for you, a big load, and here it comes. Get ready! Oh yeah! Oh yeah! Oh yeah!" I stifle a laugh.

Fortunately, he can't see my smirk at his ludicrous monologue. I want him to finish what doesn't at all feel like an act of worship. The thrusts are longer and slower. "Oh **yeah**! Yeah! Yeah! Yeah! Ohhhhhhh." There's a side to side bump and grind with the final shudder. Very satisfied with himself, he bragged, "I really wet your pipe!" I guess that means he's claiming the load was a big one, though I thought that if there was a pipe, it was inside him, what the load pumped through...

He pulls out and then cries "Oh shit! You got shit on my boots."

With mock concern I turn and look down. My cum is splattered on the floor with several gobs on his left boot. "No, no. Only on one. And it's cum, not shit." ("It was shot from the front, not dribbled from the rear," I want to add, but forebear.)

"OK: there's sticky white goop on my boot."

"You just told me there's a lot more up my bootie," I observe slyly, wondering if he's going to demand that I lick my jism off the snakeskin.

"Yeah? Well here's some of your own back," he exclaims, and wipes the boot on my inner thigh.

I suppress a laugh. I'm vaguely disgusted, vaguely titillated at the thought of licking my own cum off where I targeted it, but I'm not about to tell him that it's there deliberately, or to share my thoughts about submission and divine appetites. If he did not notice that I lost interest between "Don't move" and "Don't cum yet," so much the worse for him—

Ever eager to be a good host, I console him: "The bathroom's through the other door. You can wipe it clean there."

He's lost interest now, too. He's had what he came for and mentally he's already gone. He says vaguely, "Yeah, OK," not "You put it there, you get down and clean it up." I would have wiped his boot with a Kleenex—unless he had insisted on my tongue—The very disgust titillates me. (No use in being squeamish if one doesn't get shivers of horror now and again?)

He kicks off his pants (now? I think), picks them up and carries them into the bathroom. His chocolate calves bulge above the light-colored boots. I'm surprised that he was wearing underwear (black-and-red-striped boxers). I'm not surprised that his cowboy hat is still on, since I never heard it land anywhere. I like the idea that I've been ravished by someone too intent on doing the deed to take off his boots or hat. All that's missing are spurs on the boots—

Before the door closes, I notice that he has a bubble butt himself. Water runs in the sink. When I sniff the towel later, I can't distinguish his cum from mine, if, in fact, both are mixed there.

I thought he might take the other door from the bathroom and leave that way, but he did come back through the bedroom, dressed. I debated whether to clean up the mess and whether to adjust my attire. Eventually I decided to wipe the cum off the floor, take off my shoes, but to leave my socks on, and I changed into shorts—so it would be easy for him to yank them off if he wanted a second helping. However, as I thought, his mind had left before he went in the bathroom. As soon as he shot his load, in fact...

I wasn't expecting a closing remark focused on me, so was pleasantly surprised that he noted "When you cum, you really cum all over. You got a thick dick for a white boy, too. And a re-e-e-e-huh-ly, re-e-e-ly beautiful round butt on you."

I wanted to say something about his own bubble butt, which I would have liked to fuck—I could easily have gotten it up if he'd been willing, but I didn't ask. I just said "Thanks." I meant for the compliment(s), but if he understood it to apply to fucking me, there was nothing to be served by clarification. Nor was there any reason to learn his name or occupation now. His smile was polite rather than lustful. I was relieved that there was no more gratuitous rudeness.

He did not pause to run his hand up my thigh and under my shorts. I don't think he would have stopped if I'd been naked, lying on my stomach, spread-eagled. He might have commented on a hard-on, if I'd displayed it, but he got what he sought and now was eager to fly off to the next honey pot he could find—or to sting some other slightly ajar pink rose—or, perhaps, go to a job somewhere.

I took a hot bath for my somewhat ragged bottom. I imagined particles of shit and blood and cum in the bathwater and showered before getting out of the tub. And I wonder why I was titillated by the thought of licking my cum off his boot. Am I going to start finding humiliation hot? Have I already? Should I consider being taken to be "humiliating"? Not unless I consider it humiliating for those whose asses I take.

Do I? No.

And I don't like taking orders, especially the "Don't move" one. That is definitely not eroticized humiliation for me. It's OK to treat me as a wanton, one who wants it, but not as an inert object————but he sure could drive his tongue in, I remember fondly. The way he ate my ass made my ears ring and my toes curl, and I wouldn't be surprised if my hair stood on end, too. I'd never before realized or guessed that tongue-fucking could be a religious experience! Whatever disenchantment followed, and however quickly...

Back on Top

I was in New York doing archival research. I left the archives in midtown in mid-afternoon, and was looking at classical music, when I glimpsed Jesse looking through Rossini operas. He glanced at me briefly, then back at the (vast) array of Rossini. I continued to look at him. He glanced at me again, looked quickly down, then slowly back up.

I can't imagine why I didn't want to talk in the store, but I led him outside, looking back several times to make sure that he was following.

Outside, he spoke first, "Jesus, no one has ever cruised me like that!"

I doubted it. He had a wasp waist, swelling chest, swelling ass, solid legs, long eyelashes, and slender, curved eyebrows. I was ready to do whatever he wanted. He suggested we go to his apartment on the upper east side (84th Street).

Vocal, choral, and opera recordings covered one wall of Jesse's living room. Built-in bookcases lined his bedroom. A hardcover first edition of Christopher Isherwood's *Exhumations*, which I had never seen before in a private collection, caught my eye. Jesse had all the gay books I had, plus many more.

I didn't have time then to inventory his collections of either books or recordings. While we were kissing, he was greasing himself, and I was in him before I knew it. A rhythm was set quickly, and I came pretty quickly. He did not complain, but I sensed that he was disappointed. "Don't worry, there's more where that came from. It's like oolong tea: the first cup is a throwaway."

"So I've heard," he said skeptically. He started to get out of bed, but I pulled him back.

"Believe me! We've only just begun."

He relaxed and started playing with my balls. When something stiffened above them, he smiled, and commented, "You recover fast. Is this for me?"

It was. Slower. And repeated again. And then we went out for dinner. When we returned we resumed.

"Can you just keep doing that?" he asked after I'd fucked him five times.

After two more, he said, "I believe you! Let's get some sleep and then start over in the morning."

He didn't have to go to work, but I had a 10 o'clock interview and then I had to go to Washington for more interviews and more archival excavation. But the next weekend, I could spend in New York if I had someplace to stay. He invited me to stay with him.

After letting me in his apartment on that Friday afternoon and giving me a set of keys, he had to go out for a while. That was when I was able to inventory thoroughly his collections. I compared several recordings of Mozart's Requiem. When he returned, he said he had another appointment at 9, but wanted me to fuck him before we had dinner, and then, if I didn't mind, to return to his apartment around 10:30, or if I wanted to go somewhere else…I was content to sample disks and browse through his library (and large collection of playbills).

I was reading *On the Frontier* in the bathtub when he returned. Jesse sucked me off while I was still in the tub. (I did stop reading.) Then he got in with me. Then he wanted to crouch on my cock. This was not feasible in the bathtub, so I sat on the toilet and he squatted on my lap, facing away from me, impaling himself vigorously.

I reached for his cock, which was limp. He brushed my hand away.

The phone rang several times during the night, but Jesse did not answer it.

In the morning, after serving bagels and lox and coffee, he was teaching me how to play backgammon—irritated that I won several games—when the phone rang. Jesse said "Yes" a number of times. After he hung up, he asked me, "Could you find something to do for a few hours? I have to meet someone here—"

"No problem." I wondered if there was a lover I didn't know about. But one who was only going to drop by for an hour or two? That didn't seem to make sense.

"There's something I haven't told you about myself," Jesse said, sucking in his cheeks and lips.

"Yeah? What?"

"I'm a callboy."

"I know," I blurted out. I had not consciously known, but it made instant sense of his less-than-predictable movements and lack of a work schedule, and the numerous phone calls.

"You do?" he asked, puzzled. "And it doesn't bother you?"

I thought about that and decided, "No. I think it's sort of exciting that someone who has sex for money wants to have sex with **me** for pleasure."

"You give me lotsa pleasure," he said earnestly. "So much that I don't mind the income loss from your being here."

Having only just realized, as he said it, that he was a callboy, I had not thought about that. "The calls you didn't answer?"

"And some that I did. You've cost me plenty, but it was worth it!"

"Was this a regular, who just called?"

"Yeah. A good tipper. We'll have lunch on his tip."

"Do your customers fuck you, too?" Do they do the things I do, I was really asking.

"No. They want a big black stud—"

"You?" I asked, incredulously. Besides having been a total bottom with me, wasn't he too pretty to be a stud?

He laughed very loudly. "They don't know me. All they know is that there is a big black dick for them. That's all some of them see, and all that most of them want. I'm just around to supply it with blood and to aim it at and into them."

"And that's why you don't like me touching it? It's your livelihood, I mean?"

"What I really want is what you do: top me over and over—"

"Like you do your customers?"

"Yeah. I mean I suck some of them off."

"But none fuck you?" I hoped.

"Hardly ever—and none like you."

"Well, I need more than an hour to do what I want to do."

"Oh some pay for a whole night, but no one delivers as often as you do."

Should this flatter me, or was it an indication that I should I be renting out my potency? Not to Jesse, of course.

I kissed him, and then told him, "I like you no matter what you do when I'm not around."

He beamed. "You're not jealous?"

"About what?"

"OK, I'm not trying to convince you to be. Just that some gentlemen do not want to consort with a prostitute—"

"I think that many gentlemen pay for the privilege. No?"

He laughed. "You really are something else."

"A scholar, but no gentleman?"

"A smart boy with a stiff prick—and a good heart."

I thought it was supposed to be the prostitute with a heart of gold, not the john who loved her. Did I say "love"? I felt very comfortable with Jesse. He was a little too passive in bed, but we could talk about books and music. He knew a lot more than I wanted to know about opera and recognized my preference for the more choral and ensemble ones (such as "Die Zauberflöte," "Mefistofele," "Khovanchina," and "Four Saints in Three Acts"). And he was spending money that he earned from renting himself to take me out to my first Broadway play that night, so I was not just his back street boy. If I had to leave for a few hours, that was no great imposition.

If I'd lived in New York or he in San Francisco, would our one night and one weekend have been as intense as they were? Probably not. He wrote marvelous letters about Manhattan culture and—if they two can be distinguished analytically—Manhattan gay life.

I didn't make it back to New York for some years. Jesse wrote me that he was going home to Jamaica and was going to teach music in a school there. I could not understand how someone whose primary interests were the Metropolitan Opera and Broadway plays, and who seemed to like white dick, could live in Jamaica. I received one card (with no address) from Jamaica. And a few years later when I was in Manhattan for a meeting, I called his number, which by then had been reassigned to someone else. In the interim the thought had occurred to me that he had settled down somewhere in the vicinity of New York City and only said that he was moving back to Jamaica. (Even the other Jamaica was hard to credit: he was so thoroughly a Manhattanite.)

I met a few people who traveled in the gay art and music milieu on the edges of which he had traveled (no doubt penetrating some of the central figures!). Those who remembered him did not know what had become of him, however.

The Real Thang?

A friend I had met at a professional meeting in San Francisco called to ask if I could house an African protégé of his who was coming to see Sodom-by-the-Bay. He was from the Gambia and his English name was Richard.

He was short and very visibly hung. I mean he dressed to advertise the substantial bulge that was his crotch. He got in fairly late on a Wednesday night. There were not many people in the Castro. He was delighted that there was a black gay bar and that I bought him a late dinner.

I had made up the living room couch for him before he arrived. When we got back to the apartment, I issued him a towel and wished him good night.

The next day we went to Muir Woods, confirming Ronald Reagan's comment that when you've seen one redwood, you've seen them all. Not that I want them clear-cut, but I much prefer Muir Beach. It would never occur to me to think that when you've seen one wave, you've seen them all. Waves are infinitely fascinating to me. To each his own.

After dinner, I wished him good night and was about to go to my room, when Richard asked, "Don't you like me?"

In that I'd taken off the whole day to show him around Marvelous Marin, the question surprised me. "I do. Why would you think I didn't?"

"Because you don't want to take me to bed with you?"

"I don't? I thought you were only into black men."

"I could get into you!"

"Could you? I don't like to suck cock."

"Me neither, but what about that ass of yours. I think it's very sweet."

"Um, thanks, but, um, you're so big. I don't think that I could take what you have."

"Oh, you could! You **could**. And enjoy it! I'd feed it to you nice and slow—"

"I don't know. How about if I fuck you instead?"

"Only my husband fucks me!"

"You're a faithful wife?"

"Yeah, nobody but Rodolfo fucks me."

"And do you fuck Rodolfo?"

"No. He jerks me off while he fucks me."

"And you want to fuck me—"

"Yes, I most certainly do, if you'll let me. You have lubricant?"

"Of course."

"Why don't you put some up your ass and sit on my cock. That way you can set your own pace."

He had his pants off instantly. I couldn't possibly take all that! How was I going to extricate myself from this encounter?

He played with himself while I lubricated. I slowly impaled myself, though because of my impatience, not slowly enough. Richard smiled encouragement: "That's the way. You can do it. Take your time. It's not going anywhere else. Yeah. That feels good, doesn't it!"

Not really, but, astoundingly, inch after inch of slid inside me until, finally, it was all inside. I began to swivel gingerly around it—I mean on it.

"See? I told you it would fit. Now, we're going to turn over slowly, OK?"

When I landed on my shoulders, I straightened my legs, starting to wrap them around his neck. Richard had another plan. He put my legs together and moved them like an upside-down pendulum, grinding his cock inside me. I was startled that there was a position I hadn't tried before.

After winding the key in the lock for a while, he asked, "You know it can go in now, right?"

"Somehow it went in, yeah."

"It fits. You could rotate on it, but I'm going to pull out. I want you to turn over, so we can do it doggie-style."

In fact, it did get back in, though hardly without resistance. I liked it well enough to bring myself off while he fucked me from behind.

After we'd both come and cleaned up, Richard went to sleep on my shoulder. I slipped out of his embrace in the morning and made breakfast. After we'd had breakfast, he asked me, "Do you want some more of what I have?"

Truthfully, I replied, "I'm sore from last night and couldn't possibly take any more."

Slyly he responded, "You could, but only if you wanted to. To take what I've got, you have to really want it."

That night he went to the Pendulum and did not return until Sunday afternoon, shortly before his ride was picking him up.

I received intermittent letters from him about his studies and various problems. The primary one, "la migra" (the INS), he resolved by marrying the sister of his boyfriend. He told me about his breakup with the Brazilian who had been his "husband," but I heard from others about the boyfriend and his sister. Another friend who had had an affair of some months' duration with him opined that Richard had plenty of dick to satisfy brother and sister, and was certain that he was doing so (contradicting the account of roles Richard fed me...).

Too Young for Love?

Chuck had a will to be remembered. Usually, he delivered his cock, but would do anything so long as he believed he wasn't just a trick. Which was too bad, since he was perfect as a trick—

"I looked up the hill," he said, "and saw those hairy legs stickin' out of those tight shorts. And I liked your beard. I thought, 'Why does he have to be straight? No one who looks that good should be straight.'"

I had been surveying the bushes on the eastern slope of Buena Vista Park. A young but frumpy woman who came up beside me was interested in a longer vista. She was trying to frame a photo one-handed as her cocker spaniel jerked the other hand, so I offered to hold the leash while she took her picture. This scarcely distracted my gaze from the black figure on the stump immediately below us. He motioned to the gnarled shrubbery behind him.

"You were with that woman, but you were so cute! It didn't seem fair for her to flaunt you in the fag park. I gave you a Fonzie 'Hey!' sign, because I really liked how you looked. I never thought you'd come down!"

"I thought you were motioning me into the bushes."

"No! I was **not**. Your legs turned me on, and I just wanted to show you that I liked how you looked. I never thought you'd come running down the hill and almost get run over jus' to get to me! I saw you walk away from the edge, and I thought that was it—end of da show—but then there you was in front of me all of a sudden and the almost being run over by that car!"

"I was **not** almost run over by the car, and I did **not** come running down! It's a steep hill, and I climbed down as slowly as I could. I was completely stopped when I reached the road, and I waited for the car to pass before I started to cross it."

"But, you never took yur eyes off me, and I didn't think yuh saw the car," he sputtered.

"Of course I didn't take my eyes off you, but that doesn't mean I didn't know where I was going or where I was. Haven't you ever heard of peripheral vision?"

"No. What is it?"

"Never mind—and then?"

"Then you were right in front of me, and I couldn't believe it. I couldn't believe you were interested in me. Remember, I thought you was straight, and then here you is. I mean, I didn't want sex, I just liked the way you looked—"

"You've mentioned that—"

"And your shorts were even tighter than they looked when you were on the top of the hill, and I really got off on looking at you."

"You could have told me that—"

"I could **not**! And what did I say? 'My, aren't we fast?'"

"I thought all that was already worked out when you signaled me to come down, motioning into the bushes—"

"**No**! I did no! I was just saying, 'Hey, you looks good.'"

"Well, I thought you'd suggested the bushes already, so after I said 'Hi,' I was just accepting your invitation to accompany you to the bushes—"

"And I said, 'My, aren't we fast!'"

And I'd said "No," and then listened to a long disquisition about how tired he was of men just being interested in him long enough for him to fuck them. Since the sun was behind me and blinding him, I put my sunshade over his Afro. The gesture, which, for all I know, was spontaneous, charmed him.

Close up, I could see the classical perfection of his body beneath his loose clothes. If I was going to have him, it would have to be elsewhere, not in the park.

My lust had been immediate from the distance, and the effort and the opportunity for closer scrutiny had only intensified it. "If you don't want to go into the bushes with me, maybe we could meet for coffee—"

"I don't drink coffee," he replied unhelpfully.

"—or have a date, or you could come to dinner. I live not very far away. Would you like to come for dinner? You'll have to watch me cook first—"

"Can't I help?

"Ah, ummm, sure."

As we descended from the park, he claimed that he had not been poised at the edge of the fucking and sucking area in order to cruise, but to draw and to write. To prove this, he showed me his notebook (filled with childish scrawl), an empty sketchbook, and a book on drawing faces. I remained unconvinced by these props for lengthy stays near the heart of cruising grounds. So many men so often pretended to be there for other purposes, but were obviously "loitering with intent" to connect for sex.

The apartment tour culminated in the bathroom. Since I'd shown myself interested in more than quick sex (not only by bringing him back home with me, but by starting with my bedroom and actually continuing the tour), he rewarded me with what I wanted, which was sex. Before going to bed with me, however, he wanted to shower. Once his body was unveiled, I could scarcely wait for such niceties. He thought that **I** was cute???

"But what's so cute about me?" he asked when replaying our first afternoon.

"Your soft kinky hair, your bubble butt, your defined chest, your tight waist—"

"My cock?"

"Your cock is nice, too—not cute, exactly, but I like how it looks."

"How it **looks**?" Genuine puzzlement, not coyness, I judged.

"Yeah, how it looks: very decorative. It's too big to be of any use"—but I would soon discover that I like to feel it flop like an eel out of water when you sit on my cock, or to look at it lying in wait between your spread thighs when I mount you, or to watch you milk it onto your belly or mine with your look of intense concentration—but how can I tell you these things?

He could have retorted, "Other men find it has some uses," but I think that he was relieved—after so many slobbering size queens—to have it devalued, and other assets praised.

"I like to look down at where your waist narrows, and at where your butt surges up, or up at you wriggling onto my stake—"

"—or sideways, or upside down—"

"—or sideways, or upside down," I agreed. "I like to look at you from any angle, any time. And I like to feel the heat of your body—"

"What heat? I always feel cold!"

"You shiver from keeping your thermostat set so high."

"What can I do about that? How do ya turn it down?"

"There's nothing you can do about your metabolism, but, to stay warm, I'd wrap a warm body around you."

"Yours, I 'spoze."

"It will serve the purpose nicely."

"Do you think your fur keeps you warm? If I was hairier, would I still feel as cold?"

"Mainly, it's that your body heat is so high, you lose a lot—"

"Seriously?" he asked skeptically

"Seriously," I reassured.

"Come onnnnn!"

"Really!"

"But why?"

"I don't know. You're just a hot man, I guess, and need to get used to it."

At least I was plenty hot for his body—whether spread-eagled below me, or squatting above me, his body seemed to come to a point at his waist, where the triangle of his shoulders and the triangle of his hips joined. Between the bulging thighs and swelling chest and shoulders, the slenderness of his waist was scarcely credible. And his buttocks were so firm that it seemed they could not be rounded, because, for me, to be rounded is to be soft. His buttocks were as hard as sun-baked tropical earth—which, also, does not seem to be rounded, but is. Two hard, black hemispheres pressed against my belly, as I pressed my thrusts to the heart of Africa, or at least at the heart of Chuck.

More accurately, Chuck's heart was thrust at me. I was not seeking it, and it was far too heavy to carry on my voyage through life, a gift that, if I accepted it, would pull me down. As it was, I was dragged down much deeper than I wanted to dive. I could "exploit the natural resources," but the upkeep was unacceptably high. Like a colony?

To switch metaphors, rather than a weight pulling me down, his love was like a typhoon, lashing me through his considerable past and present travails.

That first afternoon, I did not notice any clouds. Chuck was preoccupied with the fear that when Katherine arrived, she would drive him out, pounding on his head with one of the cast iron frying pans he saw in the kitchen part of the apartment tour.

"What will she do when she finds me here? Won't she be jealous? What will she say?" he kept asking.

In my turn, I tried to keep his mouth full. My tongue there seemed to make him uneasy, but my cock there was somehow more comprehensible.

After many repetitions of inquiries that seemed compulsive (does he want to be denounced and attacked by a jealous, frying-pan-wielding Ma Kettle, I wondered), I tried to reassure him: "We won't do anything. We don't sleep together————and she's seen me in bed with strange men before."

"Why do you think I'm strange?"

"A stranger to her, I mean."

After that scenario wound down, he turned to another fantasy. He enjoyed casting me as a straight boy staying overnight in the same bed with him. First, his body pressed tentatively against mine. When I gave no sign of waking, his hand inched across my leg, circled its destination, and finally seized its prey. My eyelids shot up, and I sternly demanded to know, "What are you doing, faggot?"

He spluttered and begged me not to tell anyone. "Just go to sleep and don't let it happen again," I cautioned: a response I remembered.

He soon repeated the tentative advances to my dick. The second time, I grabbed his hand with the evidence (throbbing) in it. He quivered in apprehension. I grabbed his head and shoved it down at my crotch. "So-o-o, you're a cocksucker," I snarled. "So suck my cock. That's what you want, so get down there and get to work on it. and make sure you do it good!"

He resisted and floundered, but I held his head in place. "Just shut up and suck it, you cocksucker! Yeaaaaaaaaaah, like that——Oh yeah."

Still nervous of Katherine, even though she had not immediately attacked him with a frying pan, Chuck didn't stay for dinner after all.

"Why do you look like you're in love?" she asked (also sternly).

"Lust," I corrected.

"He's too young!"

"When I first talked to him, he sounded so jaded. How was I to know?"

"Didn't you look at him?"

"Yeah, and I liked what I saw!"

"But you didn't notice that he was very young? And you actually spent time talking to him without noticing his bulb is very dim."

"I was burning enough for two."

"Well, fine. You had a good time. Now we can get on with our lives."

"Can it be that you're jealous?"

"Hmph! Of that? I just hope you aren't going to get attached to such an obvious loser."

"Just because you don't appreciate a beautiful male body—"

"—I am, therefore, more able to notice that it houses no brain."

"Aren't you being intolerant?"

"You think it's his color? No! You need more in a man than what you consider a 'hot body.'"

"Chuck is more than hot: he's on fire—and on fire for me."

"Well, that's very nice, but he's also stupid and you are not known for your patience with stupidity."

When he did come to dinner—several nights later—he was too enthusiastic about everything: the food, the apartment, and, most of all, about me.

Finally, Katherine shot me a single eyebrow flick of "I told you he was impossible!" and told him, "I really do know how wonderful he is, but, surely there are **uh**-ther topics of conversation."

Chuck looked crestfallen. She had hit him with something more devastating than the anticipated frying pan, although he did not know quite what.

Even my urbanely scooping up the shot was no help to him. My archly saying that "I find my wonderfulness a source of infinite fascination; you might profitably contemplate the subject more often than you do" did not rescue him, but played at her level a game of which he didn't know the rules and at which he lacked the skills needed to be an appreciative spectator, let alone a participant.

"Under duressssss—" he probably didn't know what the word meant, let alone that its immediate referent was his own discourse—"I grant it." But she was not about to let up, and continued: "It's well accepted: something we already know."

"For some, it's a fresh discovery," I shot back.

I kept trying, knowing he was following neither Katherine's attack nor my defense. Although he was puzzled by what was going on, he sensed that Katherine was criticizing him and I was defending him (or making excuses for him).

I knew that she could knock him out with a single punch in the first round. That is why she should have disdained to enter the ring with him: there is no sport in cudgeling the defenseless. Therefore, it was obvious to me that to amuse herself during what she found a dreary dinner conversation, she sought to engage me in defending him without being able to use the defense "It doesn't matter what he thinks, or even **if** he does. He's a great fuck!" I could not say that in front of him (without making it untrue). In private she could still retort, "Can't you just keep him in bed, then? Keep your dick in his mouth, so he can't talk...Must we bear his 'dinner conversation'—if it can be called that?"

I knew better than to ask what she would call it.

"Fresh." She turned the word around several times, as if she had never heard it before continuing: "Ah yes. But it is easy to **discover** your charm. I mean, it's so readily available [another flick of her left eyebrow], but you must give some credit to those who can sustain **living** with your wonderfulness."

"I could," Chuck blurted out. This provoked a spontaneous shudder from Katherine, and raised my own eyebrows: he was more guileless even than I thought. I was, of course, more touched by his eagerness to please than Katherine was. She retained her focus on his inability to please with anything but his body.

He smiled lovingly at me, as her gaze toyed with him, like her cat unable to believe the good fortune of finding my parakeet on the floor—except that the parakeet would be frozen in silent terror, fully aware of the lethal paw around him.

I knew that I could stop her if I took his hand, or even smiled at him, but I couldn't bring myself to encourage his romantic fantasies. Or was it that I couldn't bear her condescending retirement from the field of verbal battle? Her satisfaction at her uncovering a wedge between Chuck and me and at my agonizing about where the path of charity lay maddened me.

As soon as the moment for rallying to his side was past, she dropped him and smiled the message: "Ah, what a relief: you're not blind to his impossibility, after all. You haven't entirely lost your mind: you know that it is lust, not love; so go ahead, and fuck him, if you must."

In bed I was angry at her mercilessness in exposing (to **me**) my agreement with her judgment. Guilt complicated my lust, even while he was singing the praises of the hair on my ass, and stroking my softer orbs. Mentally, I crossed myself, preparing my penance. "So you like my ass?"

"Yeah, like two hairy mushmellons, side by side—"

"And you'd like to get between them?"

His pupils dilated in surprise. "Uh, yeah, if you'd permit me to."

The spirit is willing, but the flesh is unyielding, I thought. "I really don't know if I can take all that, but if you want to try, you can."

He held his cock while I wriggled back onto and around it, braced on all fours. For penance, it was too pleasurable—at least after it was inside me and he was fucking me. It did reduce my guilt, however. I was not just fucking him, he was fucking me: therefore I wasn't using him, right?

After we showered together, he wanted to play the straight boy seduction game again. He was not very good at playing the straight boy role, because he accepted almost the first tentative advance and admitted that he was also interested in sex with men, me in particular, when he was supposed to snarl contempt for faggots. No imagination. We tried again, and there was the same speedy abandonment of the straight-boy role.

"I like how you do it better," he admitted. "You be the straight boy and pretend to be asleep." Instead of "catching" him moving in on my cock, I pretended to remain asleep even when he went down on me. Even when he sucked me off. Then I pretended to wake up and tell him I had had a really great dream about my girlfriend finally having learned to suck cock and given me a great blow-job.

This new extension of one of his favorite games delighted him, especially in that it did not involve any verbal abuse. Like a child, as soon as the game was finished, he wanted to start over. I told him this time to see if sitting on my cock would wake me up. I planned to switch roles afterwards and try to suck him off, but he jacked off on my chest while writhing on my cock. The "straight boy" woke up and demanded to know, "How did this get here?"

Chuck confessed that it was his. The "straight boy" ordered him to clean up the mess and he licked his cum out of my cleavage. After that, I was able to sleep for real——only to wake up early in the morning on my side and inside Chuck's fundament as it churned back at me.

I tweaked one of his nipples and he cringed, "I didn't mean to wake you up, but I just had to have you inside me again. Please don't be angry!"

I was a little concerned about blurring his favorite game into "reality," if that's where our relationship occurred. But it felt good. It felt even better after I rolled on top of him and then rotated him onto his back. When we were done, I licked his cum off his chest. He wanted to go back to sleep with my cock between his thighs, so we approximated the position in which I'd awakened.

My ongoing Filipino friend/fuckbuddy/dance-partner Carlitos nearly flipped out with jealousy: "I can't keep seeing you! It just bothers me too much that you're in love with a nigger."

"I hate that word—"

"'Cause you're a nigger lover!"

"Don't call him a 'nigger!' I don't call you a 'Flip'—"

"But you like to flip me over. You don't want to marry me, and then you fall in love with some ignorant young jungle bunny? I can't believe it!"

"I'm not in love, only lust—"

"Lust is such a flamingo word."

"Huh?"

"Like the plastic flamingoes in yards, you know, such bad taste."

"But he's no threat to our relationship."

"How can you say that? I don't want to touch you when I know he's been touching you, especially knowing where he's been touching you, and that you like it. It makes me feel degraded."

"But you've known I sleep with black men sometimes—"

"Yes, I know, and each time it happens, I don't touch you for at least a week afterwards!"

"That's stupid!"

"No, you're stupid. Why do want to get involved with those tar-babies for, anyway?"

"I like them."

"But what about me?"

"I like you, too."

"That is not possible. You cannot like them **and** like me both!"

"I can so, and I **do**!"

"Well—I can't deal with it, all right? I can't tell you what to do, but I won't stand for it. I can smell him on you, and I hate it. It's like being fucked by a nigger. No! It's even worse: being fucked by what a nigger fucks."

"Would you stop using that word!"

"Would you stop being blacktopped?"

"I fuck him a lot more than he fucks me."

"And then you want to put what's been dipped in super-permalube in me? I want a white dick, not a used dipstick! You can't wipe off the stink, or wash it off."

"I thought you liked how I smell."

"I like how **you** smell! I don't like how he smells and you smell like him after you've been rolling in the tar."

"Come on! I don't sweat his sweat."

"But his smell stays on you, and I don't want any of it on me."

I placated Carlitos by going with him to the wharf. In the door on our way out and her way in, we met Katherine, who chided, "Why can't **you two** play together?"

"Because I don't play with anyone who messes with niggers," he snapped back.

"It's not his race I object to," she said gravely.

"Well, **I do**," Carlitos proclaimed. "I'm a racist, and proud of keeping up standards." Of course, that made me snicker, thinking of the men I found very unappealing whom he drooled over.

As we descended the stairs, I asked, "How do you know what the men in the tearoom do before you do them?"

"They stink with the white man stink, or they smell like fish, not chocolate."

"I prefer the chocolate smell."

"We knooooow you do: that's the fucking **prob**lem!"

I looked at film books while Carlitos sat in his tearoom, sucking every available white dick. After an hour or so—four men by his way of reckoning the time—I extracted him: "Want some coffee with your cream?"

"We went to Portofino and sipped cafes russes while watching a pastel sunset.

"I just think it's thrilling that you come along while I go to the tearoom and don't mind that I'm sucking other men's dicks. I've never met anyone like you before—though there was a man in there with hairy legs like yours.

"Did he have a beard?"

"Oh, yeaaaah!" His eye bulged and he licked his lips.

"And did he taste good?"

"No." This question spoiled the memory. "It was too sour, not salty like yours—but at least he didn't have no nigger smell on him!"

"You're way too concerned about color, especially the color of who I go to bed with."

"Hmph!"

"Look at that man over there and don't think of his color. Don't you think he has a nice body?"

"It's black, so how can it be nice? The color's nassss-tee. The smell will be nasty. And the personality's nasty, too."

"As if you know anything about the personality of the men you suck off!"

"At least I know that they are white and hairy!"

"At least we don't compete. I always wanted the ones who were interested in Lee, and my envy of him attracting those I was attracted to did our relationship no good."

"You're welcome to all the black and brown ones!"

"Thanks."

Leaving the black population to me, Carlitos dropped me at Hyde and Geary. As I walked up Geary to the address Chuck had given me, a plummeting jar of Hot Lube just missed my head. A skinny queen with flaming red hair leaned out a second-story window, apologizing profusely. Reassured that no one was throwing things at me, I joked, "I thought it was a come-on."

"Well, if you **want** to interpret it that way—" the queen cooed.

"I'd like to, but I'm late," I consoled.

"Next time."

"Next time try a less dangerous way to get my attention, OK?"

"OK," she laughed. "Like this?" She opened her robe. She had red pubic hair, too—and a large male organ.

"That looks pretty dangerous, too!"

"I never use it, but it's such a comfort knowing it's there."

I threw the tube back and continued on my way.

As I was suffering through watching "The Omen" on tv in a stuffy tenement studio apartment, the red queen started to seemed more attractive to me, and I regretted not tarrying. Even worse than the movie itself, was the explication of every allusion to Revelations in it, from the young "dirty old man" on whom Chuck was crashing. Bill was 22, pasty, and balding rapidly. He was a fundamentalist Christian. He was also a bitter, viper-tongued queen. He had served in the army in Germany. He made almost nightly calls to a boyfriend in Munich, while uncomfortably managing his unreturned (and, I think, unconsummated) lust for

Chuck. His envy of me was apparent—I had what he was paying for and not getting, or not getting much of—but was sufficiently polite to resist the provocations of more of Chuck's naive praise for my good looks to lash out about my age (pushing 30). He contented himself with Chuck's rapt attentiveness to whatever eschatology he chose to reveal. The movie was numbingly boring, though not sufficiently to make the exegeses bearable. I drank red sugar water, grimly wondering if it was Jonestown Kool-Aid.

Eventually (seemingly weeks later), the movie ended and we retired to Chuck's bed. It completely filled a walk-in closet. I was less than overjoyed at the lack of ventilation. The proximity of Bill—on the couch where we'd sat watching "The Omen" that turned out to be a pull-out sofa bed—also bothered me, even though there was more privacy here than in many other places where I'd fucked.

Chuck went out of his way to exaggerate panting and moaning under my thrusts, driving Bill to the bathroom and the consolations of his vibrator.

"Sitting on the toilet with your toy up you again?" Chuck railed, when he heard Bill returned to his bed. I winced at the unnecessary cruelty.

"Dahling, you already have the only **man** in the house inside of you. He can't be two places at the same time—"

"And you **do** need to fill your butt with something, dontcha!"

"What's it to you?" He wasn't going to show any pain. Nor, alas, was Chuck going to cease inflicting it, ignoring my look of displeasure, perhaps because I also tried to get his mind back on what we were doing by thrusting more vigorously into his behind—

"If ya can't get somethin' that's alive, can't you at least get something that's been alive?"

"Like what? Rob the morgue?"

"Nah, even the corpses'd turn away—and you wouldn't feel a carrot…What about a pumpkin?"

"What about your handle?"

"What handle?" Chuck missed the metaphor. My presence gave him some advantage in the joust (me, a trophy date?!?), but he still could only play crudely.

"I mean your cock."

"Not available!"

"Oh, no!" in mock horror. "You mean that hunk of a man's another of us women and likes to get fucked by a black woman?"

"Wouldn't you like to know!"

"How could I not know? I hear his every thrust and your every gasp."

"So you already know."

"Yeah, I know: you're getting stuffed, and I know your hands are in love with your cock."

"'Takes two hands to handle a Whopper.'"

"**That** is just why you'd be perfect for me. You could fuck me while he fucks you—"

"Shit, they could shoot rockets up your ass and they'd get lost in space!"

"You mean that if you fucked me, I wouldn't feel anything?"

"You could try a shotgun. The buckshot'd probably get lost, tho."

"And so should you. I guess you'd better stick to taking it up the ass, and put in a toll gate. That way, maybe we could pay the phone bill."

After all that, and working to a simultaneous climax despite my irritation that the whole exchange had occurred while I should have filled Chuck's head as well as his anal cavity, I was reluctant to venture out to take a piss. Need overwhelmed my trepidation. Although looking a little bitter, Bill reassured me, "Don't mind how we talk. I have a man of my own, it's just that he's a long ways away, and you two have each other right here and right now." I forgave him his earlier pedantry. I didn't want to be in a threesome with him, but I wouldn't begrudge him Chuck's dick if Chuck was willing to put it in him when I wasn't around.

That weekend, Chuck was locked out. Bill had never given him a key and was not home. I was going out dancing with Carlitos (as on every Saturday night). I told Chuck that I didn't want him to spend the night on the street, so he should just stay in my bed, to which eventually I'd return (after a good night blow job by Carlitos in his van: he didn't mind putting my dick in his mouth before, only after, it had been in Chuck...and maybe he thought I would just go to sleep when I went inside?).

Out of some very misguided sense of obligation to sing for his refuge, Chuck had tried to entertain the dykes, as I heard the next day after he'd left.

"I think your little black waif boyfriend must have been dropped on his head too many times."

"It is a genuine possibility. What now?"

"He showed us his collection of photographs, and they make **baby** pictures seem fascinating in comparison!"

"I can tell you're dying to dish—I mean tell me **all** about them, so you may as well go ahead."

"First there was picture of the street he lived on growing up—the street itself. You know? The **asphalt!** I tried to imagine you strolling down it singing, 'On the street where you live,' like in 'My Fair Lady.'"

"Very funny."

"Ahh, but that's only the start. There's more! One of the gravel by a McDonald's in Florida, and another one of a rock in Oklahoma, one of a parking lot in New Mexico, more rocks in southern California."

"Gee, they seem to have been memorable. At least you seem to remember every one."

"There were many more, and we had to hear about the location of each photograph and what he had to eat there."

"Maybe it's minimalist art," I suggested.

"**Minimal**, it certainly is, but I think it's feeble-minded!"

"Is **that** the *au courant* term in special ed. these days?"

"No, but I'm not at work on the weekend, and it fits. We were also forced to hear the story of his first—though brief—runaway to California."

"Lucky you!"

"He calls himself 'Mary' in it—"

"Huh?"

"You know: the generic queen name."

"I have heard it used that way, yes. That's how he refers to himself to you?" I was confused.

"In his story: the very tedious story of running away to California? With the very original title, 'Running away.' He wanted me to read it."

"Oh, he can write?"

"He can make marks on paper, some of which resemble words in English. The spelling is as minimal as the imagery and imagination. Does that make it minimalist art?"

I didn't deign to answer. Finally, she asked, "Are you ready?"

I groaned, "You're going to read it to me?"

"That way you'll be able to concentrate on something other than the quaintness of the spelling and punctuation. You'll be better able to appreciate the spell cast by the writing beyond it orthographic imperfections."

"Oh, like 'Melenctha,' which **you** like so much?"

"Hardly, but you can judge for yourself."

"Why start now?"

She ignored my sarcastic question and began, "'This was the first day I ever left home.'"

"A topic sentence!"

It got more painful and Katherine's rendition stressed every aberrant choice of words and phrasing.

After she finished, I warned her, "I'm not in love with him, but if the two of you keep pushing, you and Carlitos may push me into it."

"You're not **that** spiteful!"

"'Don't push, don't push, let it happen naturally. Love will surely happen if love was meant to be'—and won't if it wasn't."

"Nature is too slow for me. I want you to wake up now!"

"You've made your point—more than several times."

My eyes narrowed in unheeded warning. Katherine continued, "Really, Nicholas, let me administer an IQ test for you next time, be**fore** you bring someone home."

Irritated as I was at her relentlessness, I maintained my bantering tone: "You're going to accompany me into the bushes and administer tests there?"

"If that's what it takes to keep idiots out of the house, yes! If you can't screen your tricks adequately yourself, let me do it for you."

"You're that committed to testing? I thought you said the tests are culturally biased."

"So, add 20 points, and his IQ would still be in double digits. This has nothing to do with black culture. It's that you need help in screening out black retards."

"'Feeble-minded,' 'retards'—your veneer of professionalism is wearing thin."

"Little Chuck is wearing it thin."

"So we're going to start screening each other's tricks?"

"I don't trick."

"Ohhhhhh—I forgot. It's only your girlfriend who does."

"Not here—"

"OK, so if I let you screen who I bring here, I should be able to screen who **you** bring here."

"But I don't bring anyone objectionable—"

Before I could reply, her girlfriend danced in and immediately told me, "Them darkies shore can sing and dance."

"Her mother doesn't think it's safe for us here with a black man around. She wanted us to stay with her," Katherine told me.

"You know very well that Chuck has not the slightest sexual interest in either of you."

"And we have none in him, or his stories, or—God!—his photographs! Have you seen them, Nicholas?"

"No, but I've heard **all** about them."

"He takes pictures of McDonald's gravel!" It is **so** hard to stop either one from telling me what I clearly indicate I don't want to hear.

"Well you take pictures of your hands."

Katherine: "And you fuck retards."

"You spend your life with them? Why don't you can this talk and try to sell it elsewhere?"

"Just try to be more careful in the future," Katherine leered, semi-relenting.

Perhaps the most maddening part of all was that they were substantially right: he was not menacing or retarded, but it he was not very bright and I could not possible live with him. I rebelled against the unrelenting reading of Chuck by Katherine, her own psychotic girlfriend, and Carlitos, even while knowing of that the relationship was ultimately hopeless…

Especially with Chuck starting to complain that we never did anything but fuck. I tried to think of something to try to do together out of bed. He's said he liked horror movies, so I suggested, "What about a vampire movie?" I didn't want to mention that it was in German. A few subtitles into Herzog's colorization (purportedly a remake) of "Nosferatu," he asked, "Is it going to be like this through the whole movie? You have to read everything they say?"

Yes, not that there was much dialog.

When we stopped at Bill's for Chuck to pick up a sweater, Bill told us, "Nick should have taken me. Not only can I read, but I wouldn't have to, because I know German. This one here just pants at Germans, but doesn't know what they're saying. He, he, he, and hopes they'll get into his pants—"

Somehow, Chuck persuaded me to accompany him to the Metropolitan Community Church above Castro. My curiosity overcame my repugnance long enough to get me there, but not much longer. I was shocked by bare-chested ushers and overenthusiastic congregation participation, the raw appeals to emotions. I hadn't realized how "High Church" my background was. I did not like to be assaulted by the fundamentalist rhetoric, even if it was of gay-positive joyful noises unto the Lord, any more than to have buckets of blood wash over me with threats of eternal damnation for being who I was.

The sermon was built on "Bring in the clowns." Jesus Christ was a clown. Moses was a clone. Job was a clown. David was a clone. On and on, clowns and clones, like the rest of us human beans (human jumping beans in this congregation, I thought).

Then the song itself, sung not very well to a mawkish crucifixion skit. If Jesus was a clown, did that make the crucifixion a farce? It moved Chuck to tears. I couldn't begrudge him the consolation of religion, but it still made me shudder. (Intellectually, I know that we need allies and that we must split the ranks of the self-righteous, if we are going to survive, and that without religious legitimation no social change is possible in America, etc., but I don't want to watch in live and in person! Call me intolerant. I know of, but cannot empathize with the "spiritual needs" of my brothers who were brainwashed by Christianity before they had minds with which to defend themselves...)

I felt light-headed when we recessed to Castro Street and released a flotilla of balloons. All that fundamentalist rhetoric on an empty stomach nearly undid me. Even watching the balloons disappear didn't help. I wanted to flee. I wanted to flee Chuck and his needs and the Christian clowns and clones.

The last balloon gone to the heavenly void, Chuck saw a Tenderloin acquaintance, Kenny, a haggard 18-year-old with greasy strawberry blond hair and matching oily pale skin, walking down 18th Street. At once they began to read each other—with no sign of fresh inspirations of Christian charity on Chuck's part. Both felt it necessary periodically to assure me that what they were saying wasn't serious, that it was a game (as if camp were newly invented by their generation, instead of by my elders!).

Chuck began with an old standard: "You like a railroad track: laid all over the country," because Kenny hadn't been around lately.

To my amusement, when Chuck accused Kenny of having an affair with another "old troll," Kenny shot back that his current man was no older than I. Twenty-two to be exact. "And what do you know about what he looks like? You never seen him!"

"I know what he must look like to have to fuck somebody with as sorry an ass as yours—"

"When there are so many pretty boys on the street?" he bitterly finished the insult himself.

"Yeah! Who'd want someone what looks like he already been groun' up in the meat grinder?"

"Honey, I is the meat grinder. You stick it up, and I does the turning."

"I'd a been too 'fraid."

"Yours so lil it'd get lost?"

"Ain't nobody ever called it little before," Chuck bristled, forgetting that this was 'spozed to be play.

"Don't matter how big it is, if you don't know how to use it."

"Youze just jealous that I got my man **and** my big thang."

"Miss Thang, you ain't got no cock, just a handle men use to turn you over with!"

I flinched and herded Chuck along. He decided he wanted to take me out for a slice of pizza on Castro. His ordering for me was almost as amusing as being taken for an ancient 22-year-old, but some of the "humor" in his verbal joust with Kenny was too close to plausibility to amuse me.

Still, he was happy that I'd gone to church with him, and that evening wiggled his ass down on my cock enthusiastically to reward me. (OK, if that was the pay-off, it was worth the price in excruciation. Joy for me meant having his cock slap against my belly as he sat down on mine. Call me superficial, just call me!)

The next weekend, Katherine's gay college friend Steven was visiting us, and Katherine invited Chuck and me to accompany them to Point Reyes. Everything delighted Chuck: the elk, the deserted farms, the rocks, the sand, the waves, and the sea gulls, the sandpipers. We went off by ourselves for a while. We were sitting on a rock, watching the waves break. It must have been Steven's aura that put oral sex on my mind. Steven and I had gotten it on during an earlier visit, and he claimed that his hemorrhoids made it impossible for him to get fucked. We'd 69ed, and perhaps recalling that inspired me to go down on Chuck while he was sitting there. Since I couldn't get it all (or even close to all of it) in my mouth, he helped out with his hand, and I swallowed the cum that we co-opera-tively milked. Then he wanted to do me, but it was time to meet Steven and Katherine.

Riding in the back seat after dark, I undid Chuck's zipper and jacked him off while conversing with Steven and Katherine. Chuck didn't say a word. Indeed, he hardly breathed, terrified that they would find out what I was doing, what he was letting me do in their presence, which in his view was disrespectful. I knew that Katherine would prefer that I diddle him than that she would have to listen to him—

—and Steven would just have been amused, as he was the next day when he returned earlier than expected and walked in on me going down on Chuck again, this time sitting on the living room sofa while Chuck stood in front of me with his pants bunched around his calves. Chuck was deeply embarrassed, though Steven was quite impressed by what he saw, and would have been happy to watch more, or to do me while I did Chuck.

"That little black boy's got a hell of a lot of dick, hasn't he," Steven exclaimed later.

"More than I can take," wondering if Steve wanted to sample some of it.

"It looks like quite a treat, but he's totally smitten with you."

"Unfortunately! Don't I know it."

"You're complaining?"

"His dick is too much of what might be a good thing and he's too much of some other things."

"But you're getting yours?"

"Yeah. He's very generous with his body. Probably if I asked him—"

"—he'd give me permission to go down on you?" Me? Not him? Ohhhh—

"You don't have to get his permission to have that."

"Yeah?"

"Yeah."

"I have yours?"

"Yeah."

Steven knelt and took out my equipment and deep-throated it. I didn't need more sex, but any allies in managing Katherine were welcome, and especially welcome if they sucked my cock well. Such an obliging fellow I was!

Chuck came back and stayed the night. In the middle of it, he woke, terrified by a drunken black woman wailing in the street. He was certain that it was the ghost of his mother and that she was going to "get" him for telling me what she and his father had done to him as a child. "She tole me if I tole anyone, she'd come an' hurt me bad, even if she was already dead." I turned on the light, and told him the wailing was not his mother's ghost but a live drunk in the streets, but he refused to look out—or to believe me. I stroked his back, careful not to trace the welts of the visible scars. How could I let him down without joining the ranks of those who had hurt him, hurt him bad physically, hurt him even more emotionally?…

"Just because I'm too young to get into the bars doesn't mean I'm too young to love!"

"I've never confused love and the bars and never looked for love in the bars," I remarked with what I took to be urbanity and trying, as usual, to defuse the threat of seriousness.

"People are always telling me I'm too young. I want to scream when I hear it!"

"So scream! What we mean is that we are different—"

"Like black and white, right? Different. But you—all of youze—what you really mean is that you're better."

"No, only that we have had more experiences. They may not have been **better** experiences, but at least some of them are unique to us and our time. There are advantages to being young."

"Like what? Name one!"

"Being desired."

"That's an advantage?"

"I think so, and some day when you aren't, you may think so, too. Now you take it for granted."

"You don't get desired?"

"More than I did when I was 18." Woops.

"Well then—what does it have to do with being young?"

How annoying to lose a point—any point!. I could have put him on the defensive by claiming that he was calling me old, but instead I tried to explain: "People who are my age have had certain experiences you haven't lived through. I've been 18, but you haven't been 19, 20, or 29. Where were you when John Kennedy was shot?"

"I don't remember it, but I was alive, you know."

"Alive, but not toilet trained, and you didn't know what was going on in the world. We were formed in other times."

"I don't like 'my times.'"

"Neither do I."

"But I can't help when I was born and what I missed that happened before I was born. I didn't choose when to be born. I didn't choose to be born at all!"

"I know that."

"So, why should I be punished for it."

"Who's punishing you?"

"You guys: everybody who tells me 'You're too young.'"

When I was 18 and 19 years ol', those who were 20 to 25 were crying "Don't trust anyone over 30!" It would be no consolation to tell him that, when we were 19, no one dared tell us we were "too young" for anything (except going to bars, which didn't interest us anyway). We thought we were going to take charge and forge a future different from the crumbling American empire over which Johnson and Nixon presided. Some of us even thought a revolution was imminent…And if Chuck had been alive then, would these have been the experiences he remembered? Of course, not.

"You are too young. To a lot of people, I'd have to be a dirty old man to go to bed with someone your age."

"We don't have no right to love each other?" Sometimes he was so sweet—which just made it more painful...

"To a lot of people, no. Children should be innocent. Sex is for after marriage—"

"But you don't think that!"

"No. I think that children should be able to have sex with each other. And I don't think you're a child." How smoothly I could move from love to sex ("just like a man," Katherine would say if such a conversation involved someone other than Chuck). I couldn't say, "I just want to fuck you a few more times, but I'm bored or embarrassed by you when we're not fucking." The truth would block attainment of that goal.

Although I may have been "young, dumb and full of cum" at his age, not knowing how or where to deposit the latter, I knew that I could hold up a conversation with cultured adults when I was 18. My gaucheries at his age differed from his in kind, not just in degree.

No, it wasn't his age or color. I could imagine (if not relish) taking on the task of shaping someone so young, so long as he was bright, but the raw material between his small ears was not there. If I was going to settle down again, it had to be with someone potentially eventually equal, someone I wanted to be around all the time, not just someone whose body made my hormones pump faster but whose perspectives I didn't want to listen to.

He did not cut through the blurring of love and sex I'd engineered. If I lied, it was through omission, not commission. I didn't say "I love you." I also did not say, "I couldn't love you." The latter would be more of a lie, since in some ways he touched my heart—he didn't **only** excite my libido—but we couldn't be lovers, we could not live happily ever after.

"I'm tired of being treated like a child!"

In my best patient, paternal manner, I asked, "Do I treat you like a child?"

"No, but you treat me like a housewife!"

"Oh, what do you do around the house?"

"You keep me in your bedroom—"

"Where do you want to go? You don't want to read subtitles in foreign films. You can't get into the bars and discos. Where else do I go? I took you to the Gay Academic Union—"

"Where all those old trolls drooled over me?"

"Yeah, there. I thought you would be interested to see and hear a published writer, since you say you are interested in becoming one."

"I did want to, but I didn't understand what he was talking about."

Not that Felice Picano had been cerebral! I thought that he was a hack and *The Lure* implausible trash, but he talked about adult concerns, not the fantasy world of ghoulish families and sadistic teachers—or even adults preying on innocent children's vitality or bodies.

Picano wrote like Proust when compared to Chuck. Chuck and I did not live in the same universe of discourse. Our tight connection of cock to asshole was tenuous everywhere else. I knew too well that it didn't mean to me what it meant to him (that our sexual congress was not a precursor of true love and living happily ever after). I could rationalize that learning the difference between reality and romantic fantasies was a necessary part of growing up, but deep down, I believed that I was exploiting him, or at least exploiting the illusions I knew that he was nursing. I knew that I was not the person that others of my sexual partners fantasized me as being, but somehow I felt that there was a difference between being considered a one-man gang-bang and being considered True Love, as much as I had tried to discourage the latter belief.

Was my mission in life to disillusion people? I omitted important information, but I never said anything that was untrue. I had to pass over a lot in silence—Jesus, heaven to come, our great love, tales of persecution...

"You're the only person who has ever been nice to me!" Sometimes I believed that this wasn't just a line used to gain sympathy.

Out of the Blue Smog

And, as I said at the beginning, to my surprise, Chuck survived. The least proba-
ble one!

When he called me, he told me that I was the first person who had ever cared
about him and the first person who had been nice to him. He remembered me
taking him to Point Reyes. (He didn't mention sucking him off there or jacking
him off in the car.) He remembered when I borrowed Katherine's car to pick him
up in a winter rainstorm from the indigent clinic on Ivy Street and brought him
back feverish and wrapped him up to keep him warm. He remembered when
Katherine and I came to visit him at Christmas, when he was incarcerated on a
72-hour hold for observation in a locked psych unit. He said that he still had the
globe (an ersatz replica of an antique one) that we brought him and was still
grateful that we (yes, Katherine and I) cared about him and came to see him
when he was really down and feeling alone that bleak Christmas in the hospital.

He promised to send me some photos of what he looks like now, after years of
body-building, plus a tape of his songs. He told me that he always thought of me
when he heard "Lover's Concerto" and was grateful that I took him in several
times when otherwise he would have been on the street. And he claimed that he
had recovered from his childhood abuse, that he was no longer obsessed by it
since he had gone back and confronted his father and siblings. Not that any of
them accepted any blame for how his father and mother had abused him, but at
least he'd told them that though God might forgive them for what they did and
what they ignored his mother doing, he never could.

It did not sound to me that he was entirely over those traumas, but he has a
job, and owns a house with his lover of more than ten years. Probably I thought
he was dead, right? But he was alive and HIV-negative (!!!) and would always
appreciate how I had been there when no one else was and his needs were so
great.(No recriminations about exploiting his emotions to use his body, but a
measure of guilt persists even without accusations from him.)

The undeserved praise embarrassed me, but I was buoyed to learn that there
was a survivor from before the AIDS apocalypse, someone who remembered me
more than fondly.

Then seeing Chaz that night set my head spinning faster than Chuck's globe ever could turn. Chaz looked just the same. He said that he had gotten really fat, up to 350 pounds two years ago, but started working out two hours a day. His hairline may have receded a bit, but otherwise, he looked the same.

Oh, yes, he's gay now. Yeah, back then he was messing with women, but now it's only men. He lives in Marin with a sixty-plus-year-old white lover, works in The City, and sometimes takes long lunch breaks, if I'm interested in nooners some time, since it looks as though my ass is still high, wide, and handsome...

So I shouldn't assume that out of my field of vision means the black males of my youth have dropped dead. And I can look back without the despair of my earlier assumption. At least two of those with whom I had sexual relationships of some duration are alive, well, HIV-negative, and remember our liaisons fondly—and one even hinting at resuming one! One I'd have estimated to be very unlikely to have survived, is alive and claims to be thriving. I can hope that others are, too.

Culturing Some Desire(s):
What Did It All Mean?

Splicing together my remembered sexual encounters with black men, it is obvious that most of them were comfortable only as a top or as a bottom.[1] That is, they believed in strict role dichotomization—for themselves, and also for me. In contrast, I was versatile and complaisant, taking the role complementing what the other man indicated (usually unmistakably!) that he wanted. I enjoyed reciprocity, at least establishing its possibility. At least once, I wanted to fuck each top and to be fucked by each bottoms.[2]

Latinos are the prototypes of strict role dichotomization, but in my experience it is much easier to get a Latino to switch from their usual role in anal sex[3] than it is to get an African American to do so. And the sexually receptive African American partner seems to me to be even more feminized (in his view and in the expectations of those who fuck him) than Latino *pasivos* generally are.[4]

Ten of the African American men with whom I had sex were primarily or exclusively "bottoms," eight were primarily or exclusively "tops" with me, and the only one who was routinely both insertive and receptive was only receptive orally. Two of the men, Rufus and Richard, who were eager to fuck me acknowledged (after doing so) that their "husbands" regularly fuck them. They take the "male

---

1. The casually versatile men were Chuck and Jim. Chaz undertook a token switching of anal roles, symbolically breaking the either insertive or receptive mould. He also 69ed in foreplay. Rufus and the ersatz cowboy (memorably!) rimmed me before fucking me.
2. Although I now know that role switching sped HIV infection through my community before any of us had an inkling there was a syndrome, let alone that virus, I refuse to believe that we of the gay liberation generation were wrong to attempt to break down compulsive role dichotomization.
3. Getting Latino *activos* to undertake oral receptivity is much more difficult than getting them to try being penetrated anally (in my experience and in reports by others).
4. I have no experience with transvestites of any race or ethnicity, so am only talking about those presenting themselves as male.

role" only when they "stray," so that their assholes are monogamous even though their dicks are promiscuous—or something. I couldn't ask too many questions about their anal impenetrability away from home without seeming to be pleading to gain entry. Seeming to beg for admission was inconsistent with my self-image. I don't think that getting fucked was demeaning, but seeming to plead for the chance is. I didn't think that being the penetrator makes one superior, and this belief did not alter depending on whether I was penetrating a man or being penetrated by him.

I did not (and do not) buy into the belief that fucking makes one masculine and getting fucked makes one feminine.[5] At least some of those African American males who have exclusively insertive sex with other males do not identify themselves as "gay," whereas I had the gay liberationist view that one can "take it like a man," not just give his phallus to the orifice of feminine or feminized persons, and that one should go for what he wants rather than agonize about whether what he wants might be regarded by others as feminine or feminizing.

I was willing to "take it" when the "it" was the urgency of a throbbing cock. I was not much bothered about being discarded like a used rubber after being fucked. But I was **not** willing to "take it" when the "it" was being treated as anyone's "bitch." The only time the word itself was applied to me was unmistakably **not** playful, **not** "in fun." My rapist hated white men or white people or fags or hated that he needed another person's orifices—for pleasure or domination or the dubious pleasures of contempt.

Fortunately, my worst experience was over quickly, and my sexual encounters with seventeen other African American men "in the [golden] olden days" (before AIDS) were more pleasant. Some were even ecstatic. And they lasted longer, though two of the best ones did not last **much** longer. Those two occurred in the same vicinity (within the Ritch Street Baths) and, between them, were balanced between "taking it" and "giving it up." Some other "tricks" were brief, but had preliminaries even though some had no postplay or follow-up.

I thought that the way Jack had been feminized by his ex was not just wrong, but shocking. I didn't (and don't) see any necessary connection between sexual receptivity and playing the part of a woman in everyday life. (Obviously, I lack experience of drag queens, but I have not failed to notice that black drag queens seem to be plentiful, surely proportionally more than white drag queens are.) I

---

5.   However, I realize that I was more willing to be cast in the "wolf"/"stud" role than the "punk"/"bitch" role. This suggests that I was not (am not?) entirely free of the denigration of the one who gets fucked—or, at least, that I was very aware of it.

bridled at any indication of being considered a bitch, though being regarded as a bottom didn't faze me. Also, I was less than comfortable with some of these men's willingness or even eagerness to be treated as nothing but a hole to be filled with dick.

Jonah's "teammates" and adult churchmen trained him to inertness, taking it "passively." Antonio and Jesse seemed to me underinvolved. I had no doubt that they wanted to be fucked (repeatedly), but they also had learned to go along with the "Don't move" imperative. I heard that command from several insertors, and bristled at what I interpreted as sexual selfishness. Since it is upheld by both tops and bottoms, I guess that it may have been a cultural pattern. Jeremiah sure missed out on it, if it is a norm for black males who have sex with males! When they were taking my dick, Jack and Chuck participated, if less spectacularly, and much less volubly.

Which reminds me that, while I wanted to participate by moving the rump I was "giving up" to participation, I was unaccustomed to and unexcited by talk during sex, especially phallic boasts and questions of the "Do you like this big black dick stuffed up your tight white ass?" kind. Was this a "cultural difference," too? I enjoyed the verbal foreplay, but then I wanted to "just do it," not talk about what was being done or the quality of the performance or of the anatomical parts involved. I did not see any inconsistency between wanting both "partners" to be involved in fucking, while keeping any verbalizations about it as internal monologues. Conversely, some of my sexual partners did not see any inconsistency between wanting to enhance the sex with hyperbolic verbal exchanges while confining physical movement to one.

I had experiences both directions (an overanimated bottom and some underanimated ones) beyond what I thought (felt) was an appropriate degree of patent involvement in the sex I was supplying. Plus those irritating demands that I not move!

I have recounted encounters in which there was no verbal exchange. Although we had good sex, this does not establish that our assumptions about sex or about each other were necessarily the same—or even close to each other's. When understandings were verbalized, they often turned out to be wrong, even obnoxiously wrong and/or threatening to self images. The "real world" may to a large extent be unconsciously built up on language habits, but intercultural sexual encounters—even between speakers of the same language—may proceed without either partner knowing that the other is interpreting what is said and done in ways quite other than those intended or taken for granted by oneself. I perhaps took "jive" and "sweet talk" too literally in some cases, and my laconic WASP way of speaking may have struck some African Americans as a kind of uptightness or "inertness," not unlike what seemed to me to be physical inertness of some of my sexual partners.

Why did these men attract and excite me? Mostly because they were—or, at least, seemed to be—attracted to me. Rufus and Chuck thought that I had cruised them first, but mostly I responded to desire. Not unlike Chuck, I wanted to be wanted, and was willing to adapt to the sexual scenarios of those who wanted me. Unlike Chuck, I did not require appearances of love or even the possibility of love developing from the sex. What mattered was being desired by a man, not any particular attributes, such as penis size or skin coloration. Some modicum of masculinity. No drag queens. I guess I was guilty of the "no fats or femmes" exclusion that appears in sex and relationship want-ads. I did not draw any black men with less-than-average-size dicks, and they all had substantial, mostly high-jutting rear-ends, but I think this is like saying that they had thick lips and wide noses. That is, these are general racial characteristics. The one that turned me on was their rounded, ample asses. The same reason I like to watch professional football. I love to look at those bubble butts, and I used to love to fuck them or knead them while I was getting fucked by someone with one…And their legs. I do not think there is a racial type of legs, but definitely I appreciate solid, fairly substantial thighs. And these men mostly had them. Smooth or hairy, I didn't care though more were smooth than were hairy.

More notable to me now than it was then (when it was present but inchoate) is that my sexual relations with black men did not lead to participation in black circles, except for the brief entrée following the night spend with Shahid. Chuck and Jonah told me about their pasts—perhaps imagined, or at least embroidered past—in all-black social worlds, but none of these men introduced me into any predominantly black social circles. I only met white friends or acquaintances of Jim, Jack, Chaz, Richard, and Chuck. Choosing me as a sexual partner indicates that these men were not racially endogamous sexually. Those making quick exits after "the deed was done" may have not been interested in interracial homosociality. My limited observation of those who talked afterwards is that they were comfortable socializing with white gay males, not just using us as sex objects (whether the sex object of interest to them was an orifice or a phallus). Black gays. The gay blacks either ignored me or moved quickly on after sex or avoided settings that were not all-black

I fancied myself being in a state beyond jealousy. That was part of being "liberated," right up there with not being "fixated" on one role or another or "into sexual ownership of a human body." Some of us really talked like that, back then, when we fancied that we were liberated examples of "the New Gay Man." With "the return of the repressed" (drag and the word "queer" and the fascination with "performing" gender), gay liberation feels like a wave of the past, and our numbers were more than decimated by HIV.

Before the phony (and oftentimes fatal) AIDS-prevention message of monogamy began to be preached (and the "gay agenda" became Republican, suburban marriage more monogamous than heterosexual suburban marriages are...), I was not eager to learn how many other dicks were welcomed where mine was going or had gone. I entertained no illusions that the dicks that came my way were only for me. Or that they could be only for me, if I wanted monopoly rights to them. Perhaps Chuck's. He might have been monogamous with me for a while, perhaps even for a long while. But he was too young and needy and innocent not to succumb to a line about love or need from someone else. And he was not a conceivable spouse. I thought that my friends' condescension toward him was as much based on class as on IQ. Of course, they did not have direct experience of what a good fuck he was, but they **should** have noticed that he had a big heart. (He wore it on his sleeve, but also unmistakably was trying to be trustworthy, loyal, helpful, friendly, courteous, kind, brave, clean, and reverent, even though he had not been a Boy Scout.) I knew that he had a big heart that he wanted to give to me...and that he desperately wanted to please me out of bed as well as he did in it. I also knew that he couldn't, and regretted my inability to give him the haven that I thought he deserved. However, I was barely able to take care of myself. I couldn't undertake trying to cure him of his abuse as a child and adolescent. What would we have had when the sexual heat cooled? No shared interest, no shared friends, not even a shared interest in sex, which for him was the road to being held.

Was any of these men a possible life partner? It had to be someone I could talk to beyond sex talk. Probably a college education was prerequisite, or, more importantly, at least some interests (Jeremiah and Antonio had college degrees, but I don't think that either one had opened a book since then: other than sex and conventional American food, the only interest I could detect in either of them was in how they dressed). Better still, some shared interests of one kind or another...

Richard was already married, and he had a (maddening-to-me) third-world sense of time (or rather lack of concern about clock time) that would have made a relationship impossible for me, even if we had lived in the same city. Despite the disruptions of his profession, I can at least imagine living with Jesse. But besides his line of work (its irregularity as much as its nature would have bothered me in an ongoing relationship: eventually I would have wanted to "save" him from what I did not consciously consider a "life of sin," but...), he lived on the other coast.

Jim and I also had some shared interests, but we were not sexually compatible. We did spend some time together, and I was comfortable being with him except when we were going at each other physically. I liked him and wanted to please him. I think that he liked me and I know that he pleased me (not just below the belt).

I should have called Julius. Not because I was looking for a lover, but because he was likable, seemed undemanding, and I knew that he was too insecure to call me.

Before accusing, "You only fucked them [or us] but weren't willing to live with them [or us]?" remember that I was living with a gay black man (with whom I did not have a sexual relationship) and across the hall from a bisexual black man with whom I had a sexual relationship. My closest colleague was a straight African male and I worked for another. Although I was not in a gay black circle, there were black men in my social circle (which, like my many other sexual relations are not my focus here). I was not homosexually interracial and homosocially intraracial. I lived, and worked, and fucked multiculturally, multiracially.

I am sure that I was **not** screening out possible spouses because they were black. Rather, I was not spouse-hunting at all (then, or ever). I was enjoying meeting various people, sampling bodies of all flavors and colors. I was not ready to commit. I was enjoying exploring the City of Night after the frustrations of a long-term relationship and the heartbreak of being dumped. (Healthy as ending that relationship was in the long term, it hurt plenty at the time, which included the time of the encounters I have described here.)

While I was not auditioning to be "The One" for any one of any color, I did aspire to be different: a memorable one, a special one, somehow distinct, not just another white boy with a hard dick or legs that could be wrenched open. Or both—which in itself seemed to make me at least somewhat out of the ordinary, distinct from expectations that one was one or the other (not just that one **had** one or the other to offer).

BOOK TWO, 2002–03

o o o o o o o o o o o o o o o o o o o o o o o o o o o o o o o o o o

So why is it on Thursday that the men look satisfied?...People look forward to weekends for connections, revisions and separations...But for satisfaction pure and deep, for balance in pleasure and comfort, Thursdays can't be beat.

—*Toni Morrison,* **Jazz**

Jabba

I was so much younger then. I didn't fully realize that my (hyper?)potency was neither eternal nor inexhaustible. Now I begin to understand why the old go down on the young. We don't know if we can rise to the occasion, or stay risen, and we still crave contact with other male bodies. I remember hearing "A hard cock is good to find" back in the late-1970s, but never imagined I would ever cease to be able to supply one. Then I also did not understand that some of my appeal was supplying that scarce resource where drugs or age or earlier activities had blunted so many spears.

Since I don't like how I look, it have never been surprised that someone else doesn't find me attractive. Only in retrospect do I know that I used to have—and to exude—confidence in my potency, Only having lost it do I recognize that I took it for granted in my 20s and 30s. (I understood even less during my teens, when my potency was untested and embarrassingly persistent.)

Now well over 40, I know that I have to take what I can get and should be grateful if anyone wants me. Like Bette Davis, I look back and think, "Back then I looked better than I thought I did; I wish I looked like that now!" Our partners from "once upon a time" were less desperate and more discerning than we thought when we were grateful to them for desiring us. And I hope that I am more gracious and grateful now when anyone wants to do anything with me.

Along with my boyish figure, I seem to have lost the knack for making eye contact with black men looking for sex with someone like me. Most ignore me. My desire does not register on their radar, as it once did (whether they were interested or not).

OK, in days of old, I would have mounted the ones lying on their bellies in cubicles. And if I could count on staying hard, I might still. That eliminates between a quarter and a third of them, but there are more of them promenading and not meeting my gaze, either when we are at the same level, or when I am down in the mosh pit.

The "out-back" at the Steamworks, just off I-80 at University: The focus is like a sunken boxing ring—a pit with railings rather than a raised platform. The cocksuckers wait for cock either in the pit or in six cubicles with large holes (three oval, three rectangular) at the level of the cocks of men around the ring. That is, the studs are at a higher level, so that those servicing them can stand up and comfortably suck dick.

There is no one in the pit or in any of the gloryhole cubicles waiting to suck cock. Other than myself, there is only a very obese black man with a close-cropped goatee and black-rimmed glasses. We are at opposite sides of the walkway. I want him to go down on me. Would he be able to lift all that lard up if he knelt? How many towels had he pinned together to surround his belly?

He's not moving. We can just stand where we are, at a maximal distance from each other, or we can wait, hoping that someone else will arrive who is interested in one of us, or I can make a move. Perhaps I am more sexually versatile. Certainly, I am more mobile.

I circle to the cubicle nearest him. He turns and waddles to the partition. I can't see his belly anymore. He's lifting the towel. Unlike his body, his cock is quite lovely. It's uncut, unhard, unhuge. My tongue rims between the foreskin and the cockhead. I wonder what it feels like, this sensation I will never have. I swallow everything and roll it around in my mouth with my tongue. It is hardening. My own mutilated (that is, circumcised) cock is standing up. Am I turned on by this elegant intact cock? or by the humiliation of servicing Jabba the Hut?

Just like his belly, his balls hang very low. It is as if the weight of them has stretched the bag. They are heavy and solid, but there is almost two inches above them that seems empty airspace within the sacs. I can reach behind them, but can't reach his asshole, so I content myself with stroking, caressing, and jiggling his balls.

I can take most of his now-erect cock in my mouth. When I start to gag, I pull back and lick the head. Jabba peels back the foreskin. I lick the head some more. He sighs.

He does not try to throat-ram me. Because he is content with my ministrations, or because he has to lean backward to present his cock to the gloryhole? I am surprised that he was able to get his cock to the hole, that all that belly doesn't prevent delivering the goods to the waiting white cocksucker. Now you really are a cocksucker! This is proof that it doesn't matter what the man looks like. As long as there is a black cock, you now take it in your mouth.

But there was no one else to choose from, Mr. Censorious.

You couldn't wait? He's gross, grotesquely fat!

Jabba   117

But, sir, all I can see through the opening are his cock and balls. His balls are interesting and his cock is luscious. We're each enjoying our contact, so why do you need to rate his body?

Is it the thickness of his thighs that keeps his cunt out of reach of my fingers? or the heft of his testicles?

He isn't holding the foreskin back, and it slides on the back of my tongue. Soon he cums. Quietly. With no warning, I taste the viscous sour and salty liquid. It's lodged too far back to spit out, so I swallow it. I keep his shrinking cock in my mouth, gently rolling my tongue against the base. I lick forward and let it drop from my mouth. Then I kiss the hood that has re-enveloped it.

He reaches a hand in and strokes my beard. He whispers, "That was so-o-o-o good. Thank you."

Can he see me at all over the great expanse of his belly and through the relatively small opening in the partition?

I leave to gargle some diluted mint Listerine. I don't see him later. Someone who has learned to quit while he's ahead? Get off and get out? A savvy satisfied customer, not ever-yearning and reluctant to leave, as I am?

I had been excited by what I was doing—playing with a part that I lack, giving pleasure to someone who did not attract me. Filling my emptiness with plenitude? Savoring the fragility of the penetrating phallus? Relishing the collapse of the tower of power. When it is spent, the orifice remains. Able to take more. To take another. The cocksucker takes what he wants, exhausts his quarry, outlasts what some see as "submission" (though this is an instance in which doing the work seems to me "domination"—or at least control). This is how I think of performing fellatio now.

But I know the pleasures of getting off, too. I know that the cock is only temporarily vanquished. Even if it seems to lose every battle, it rises again, and the war goes on and on...

Later, or on another visit, I find a black man with a shaved head bobbing on the cock of an old white man. Why suck him when you can suck me, I think, ungenerously. Perhaps the man being blown thinks the same thing. Or he doesn't want to be dropped and prefers to take the initiative and retreat. Or he is holding back ejaculation for later. Or doesn't really like black cocksuckers. How do I know?

I am grateful that he pulls me over to take his place. The black man on his knees looks up briefly at my face and then lunges to swallow my cock. Looking down, I admire his long, hairy thighs. The muscles bulge as he crouches. He has a big (circumcised) cock that he is gently working.

I give him some warning in case he doesn't want me to cum in his mouth. He jiggles his head, pressing his nose against my belly to take my cock deeper into his throat. He swallows twice. I slowly retract what is left of my own collapsed tower Now I am the one who has been outlasted. Not just by his mouth, but by his cock, which he has stopped stroking, politely not pressuring me for anything.

Would I have gone down on him, if he'd kept sucking the old man?

He stood up and embraced me and thanked me. I kissed him lightly and thanked him. He grinned and said, "You have a nice cock and really nice legs."

All I could think to say was "Thanks." I could have said, "You suck good" or "I'd like to fuck that pretty ass of yours" or "Do you want me to do you now?" The first was too obvious; he had to know he was good at sucking cocks. My cock was too unreliable (not to mention spent) for the second. And I had no indication that he wanted any reciprocity. But why didn't I return the compliment about legs, especially since I had been admiring his?

Another Kind

My eyes had not entirely adjusted to the darkness, but the man I saw looked very interesting and interested. Quite dark skin for such straight hair. A bit curly. Strong, hairy legs. A dazzling smile. Not particularly thick lips. Thick eyebrows that almost grew together above his nose. No facial hair, but a carpeted well-built chest. An even thicker pubic thicket (of hair that was more curly than kinky).

We kissed, stroking each other's cocks.

"Do you have a room?" he asked.

Once the door was locked, he knelt on the floor and started sucking my cock. He did that for a brief time, then rose and kissed some more. I gently pushed him back onto the bed and knelt to take his large and slightly upward-bent organ in my mouth. He moaned as my finger pressed through his sphincter and began a constrained circumnavigation. I licked from his balls almost down to my finger and back.

"Let me do you some more," he pleaded.

I lay down beside him and we 69ed for a while.

He climbed over me and jacked off while sucking my cock. I warned him when I was going to shoot and scattered my seed in the luxuriant forest of his chest.

We showered and returned to my room. His name, Raju Raman, suggested that he was not African American, and that his hair was straight, not straightened. I guessed that he was Tamil Sri Lankan. I was too far east. His parents were from Kerala. He was born in Calicut, raised in Calcutta. Yes, these are different cities, not my mishearing the first, he assured me. He graduate from Stanford. Now (at 25) he's the youngest manager in Chevron's computer operations. He has a lover. Named Guy. White American. Exactly my age. A bottom. A *total* bottom. And HIV+ like me.

Raju had not seemed very like a top! Responsive to being fingered and eager to go down on me.

He said that he loved Guy very much and told him everything, including what he did at the baths, including how often and with whom. Raju said he'd like to be fucked by me. I wished that that was possible, that my wasted teenage potency was available now that I needed it and knew what to do with it. Of all the ways youth is wasted on the young, this could be the saddest.

I could remember when my cock would be standing up again the way his was. I suggested he stand on the bed, so I could kneel on the mattress. This time I swallowed his ejaculate.

He asked if I had something with which to write. I ripped the due-date slip from a library book that was in my backpack, and tore it in two. I gave him my home number. He gave me his work number and his cell phone number. When I saw he'd also written his e-mail address, I took back the other half to write down mine.

I went along with him to his locker. His cell phone showed that Guy had called, but he decided to wait until he was outside to return that. I loved how his blazingly white briefs and shirt looked on him. His ass filled out the back of his black slacks, too. Even the somewhat nerdy glasses seemed adorable to me. He gave me a business card, which contained less information than the slip I already had.

After he retrieved his wallet and checked out, we had a lingering kiss before he went out the door.

We exchanged some e-mails. I looked up what the primary language of Kerala was and asked how to say "I want to fuck you" and "I want you to fuck me" in Malayam. He confirmed that Malayam was his mother tongue, but, he wrote back, since he had moved away and only spoke it with family, he didn't know what the Malayam word for "fuck" is.

We scheduled an afternoon rendez-vous at my house. Since he never lies to Guy, and had told him he was getting a massage, he asked me to rub his back. I readily complied. I wanted to work my way up his legs and (unsurprisingly) I focused on kneading his buttocks. Then I was massaging his prostate. Then I was kissing his hairy orbs. Then my tongue was trying to push through his sphincter.

I hadn't rimmed anyone in a quarter of a century. As hairy as the area was, it smelled and tasted clean. I know: this is like deciding that someone can't be HIV+ because he looks healthy and therefore letting him fuck you without a condom. I know that it is magical thinking. Or magic **in place of** thinking before going for forbidden pleasures. Risky, dangerous. And for someone as squeamish as I am, how can it be pleasant? But it was. Exciting because forbidden? Perhaps somewhat. But it was mostly the excitement of driving Raju wild, the great pleasure of giving intense pleasure.

Raju was wriggling, swooning, and begging me to fuck him, but my cock did not respond to the summons. My younger self would not have believed such failure possible, but all I could do now was finger-fuck him while I sucked him off.

He then got off the bed to suck my cock as I sat at the edge of the bed. I was thrilled by the sight of him on his knees working on me. Thrilled, but not altogether erect, alas.

I knew that I could ejaculate. I liked what he was doing—especially, I liked watching him doing me. I liked it too much to take over. Eventually, I asked him to come up and kiss me and forced an ejaculation through my semi-limp dick with my hand.

"You made me work hard," he whined.

"I thought you liked it." Really, I didn't know whether he did. (In contrast, there was no doubt that he'd wanted me to fuck him.)

"I did. I'm sorry I couldn't get you off. I really wanted to"

"The spirit is willing, but the flesh is weak."

"What does that mean?" (I'm not sure that I'd thought he was Christian.)

"I think you are incredibly hot, but my dick just isn't functioning these days. When you can't get it up or keep it up, you have to be the bottom."

"I'm a top, you know. I always top Guy."

"And other guys?"

He frowned while processing that, then laughed, "Yeah."

"So why don't you top me?"

"I thought I already did."

"But it looks like you're ready for more."

"You want me to fuck you?" Why did he sound so surprised?

"It's been so long and you're so big, I don't know if it's possible any more."

"Don't worry! It's possible. [Pause] If you want it."

"I want it, but for all practical purposes I've become a virgin again." (That turned out to be truer even than I thought.)

"You should sit on it so you can control how fast—how slow—you take it."

"And you'll be able to stay hard."

"Sure." To be young…

It hurt, and I soon felt an acute need to urinate. "I'm sorry, but I need to piss."

"No you don't. You just think you do. Keep going——please."

He was right. How could I have forgotten that feeling? I remembered the initial pain and eventual pleasure, but not the confused early signal from the prostate.

After I was more than comfortable, we switched positions. My prostate continued to be confused. I felt like I was going to cum, though I wasn't hard, and didn't cum.

One more switch of position: this time onto my back. I still didn't get hard and didn't cum, but Raju reached completion looking down at me as my feet caressed the back of his neck. His mouth fell open. I could see his tongue curl and his pupils roll back in his head. Whether this indicated it was very good or took a lot of concentration, I'm not entirely sure. I guess the two aren't mutually exclusive.

He talked about his emotionally distant father and about a classmate he regularly fucked in Calcutta (not Calicut!), though his preference is for older men (like me). I recounted being in love with a high school classmate but not knowing that two males could have sex. Raju thought I must have been an idiot not to know that. An emotional idiot, I'd agree. I told him about my very late awakening with the last man whom I'd rimmed (Juan Carlos) more than twenty years earlier.

Raju reiterated that he tells his lover everything and was uncomfortable about telling him about seeing someone (else) more than once.

I again enjoyed watching him get dressed, especially stuffing his lovely, well-rounded butt into his ultra-white briefs. Of course, I regretted that I had not been able to stuff his more-than-ready butthole

For the next few weeks, he had an excuse for not being able to see me at any of the times I suggested. Not just work removing most possibilities, but some business trips. Our e-mails back and forth were salacious. He seemed to find me almost as desirable as I found him. He fantasized my fucking him. So did I. In cyberspace it was easier. And in my mind: I had a pretty good idea of what it would feel like. Thrilling is what it would be like to mount that muscular butt and thrust deeper than my tongue could into that quaking tunnel…

Perhaps six weeks later, I met him as I was leaving the lavatory at the Steamworks. I stopped. He smiled and said hi. I lingered while he pissed. He smiled again and coyly asked, "Waiting for me?"

I didn't have a room, but persuaded him to climb into the loft with me. Although I tried to be careful of the awkward curvature of his erect penis, he complained about my teeth.

He suggested we take a break and shower. I thought we were still together in the shower, but after we got out, he told me that he didn't think he should violate his agreement about not seeing anyone but his lover more than once.

I did not point out that this was a Rubicon he had already crossed. I did not follow him back to the Out Back. Later, I watched someone else suck his cock. He didn't cum. He glanced at me. Only a glance. I fancied that he forced himself to look away and had to force himself not to long for me. I hope that it wasn't easy.

The next day, the dismissal notice was in my e-mailbox:

> I am sorry. But I am in danger of getting too emotionally involved with you. Guy and I have this agreement that we be emotionally monogamous with each other. To ensure that, I must not see you anymore. I have been fighting falling in love with you, but it has been happening anyway. Hope you understand. I know that you are aware of my strong attraction for you and that I like you very much. But I love Guy very much and I don't want to do anything to jeopardize our relationship.

I thought about pointing out that I was safely coupled myself and could give him some of what he wanted and wasn't getting from Guy. Instead, I replied:

> Of course, I will not force myself on you, though I think you are the perfect concubine for me. You know very well I am intensely attracted to you! I was hoping that through chemical aids I could fuck you soon. I am sorry that I won't get the chance.
>
> I wish you the best in every way. It would be easier on me if I didn't have to see you and not be able to have you, so I hope that you will visit the Steamworks at other times than 2–6 on Thursdays, at least for the next six months.

He agreed to schedule other times to go there and I haven't seen him again. I have jacked off thinking about him, remembering him on his knees fucking me, on his knees sucking me, and imagining real penetration of his lovely butt, extrapolating from the willing if narrow opening that I had licked into a frenzy

Sigh!

"Just a little bit more" adds up

I was in the darkest gloryhole cubicle sucking the thick uncut cock of a hunky black man. He did not want to cum and stepped back. A wiry black man with a thinner cut dick and lighter skin pushed to replace him. "Youze stepping on my foot, motherfucker," the first one snarled.

"I'm sorry, but I'm trying to get in here to get my cock sucked, too." Assuming that whoever is sucking one black cock will want another one, if the first withdraws. That I took it in his mouth undoubtedly confirmed his assumption. It was average in length, less than average in girth, so fairly manageable. Circumcised, unfortunately.

We were not in a position in which I was expecting any verbal intercourse, but he asked if I had poppers (no), then: "Do you have a room?"

"Yes. Do you want to go there?"

"What would we do there?"

"I'd suck your cock some more."

"You can do that here. Do you have any toys in your room?"

"No."

Along with answering his questions, I'd managed to get his cock hard.

"Where do you live?"

"San Francisco."

"Umm."

After some more ministrations: "Don't go away, I'll be back," he commanded.

He walked around looking at other cubicles. I moved to another one. I liked the pert ass I saw as he checked his options on the other side. He was high-waisted, but not bubble-butted. His ass-cheeks were high and looked hard, but didn't especially jut out.

When he returned to the side I was on and thrust his semi-hard cock through the hole, I went back to work and, without making any audible complaint, res-tiffened his appendage.

Apparently, he did not know that the same man was servicing him again. He again asked: "Do you have a room?" I repeated that I did. After some more minutes of sucking his cock, his wanderlust returned. Again he told me "Don't go away, I'll be back."

I left the backroom altogether. Twenty or so minutes later I went into the mosh pit. Soon my slender black squirrel was standing over me and I was getting his cock hard again—or, more correctly, sort of hard. I suspected that he had cum but was not willing to rest and wait to recharge his batteries. After some more exertions, he broke away and told me for the third time "Don't go away, I'll be back." I was quite able to complete the thought: "—if I don't find a better option": trying to store away cocksuckers the way squirrels store nuts for later use.

On my next return to the backroom, I was up on the walkway. Another white boy was on his knees sucking the squirrel's dick. I caressed the black man's hard buttocks. He grabbed my semierect cock and smiled at me. The man sucking his cock was not pleased that so much attention was being directed my way. He stood up and left. The black cock-supplier guided my head down to take the previous cocksucker's place.

I don't like the idea of someone else's saliva coating a dick I'm going to suck. If I take stranger's dicks in my mouth—including the rapid succession of two of them earlier—why should de facto kissing another stranger bother me? Well, because I choose my partners and would not choose for any intimate contact the one who'd been going down on him. However, I overcame that repugnance. Why, I'm not sure. Wanting to be wanted, I guess. I think that is my prime motivation in sex.

Yet again, he asked if I had poppers (no), a room (yes), poppers in my room (no), tv in my room (no), did I eat pussy (no). Despite all but one negative answer from me to his stream of questions, he was (at last!) ready to go to my room. Probably it was that he was tired of standing up being done, though, perhaps, it was the interest I'd exhibited in his ass.

This was the first opportunity I'd had to take a good look in the light at his face. I liked it. His hairline was somewhat receded. He had a cleft chin, nearly almond-shaped eyes, a relatively long (though flared) nose, long ears. A long face, in fact. I liked the almost straight eyebrows above sly eyes. Like his butt, his chest was hard but not very concave. It was hairless. A slender ladder of tightly coiling hair rose to his navel. His thighs were nearly hairless, though some grew on his shins and below his lightly muscled calves.

I knelt over him on the bed sucking his dick for a while. Then he sat up and I knelt on the floor, a better, roomier position in which to jack myself off.

I knew from not being able to cum a second time, even from the ministrations of highly skilled cocksucking, that only I could bring myself off a second time. By the time I did, I was massaging my companion's prostate, alternating one and two fingers up his ass, alternating licking and rubbing my chin against the bulge between his spookie and the balls that were squeezed far out by a very tight cock ring. His hand was stroking the cock I had abandoned.

My back was tightening. He told me to get up on the bed but **please** not to stop, that he was close to cumming. The new position was better, if not good for my back, but stressed my neck. After a polite interval of continued exertion, I sat up, only continuing to diddle his booty. He did not cum. I said I needed to get my sore back into the jacuzzi then hit the road.

"Where do you live?" he asked (again!).

"San Francisco. And you?"

"San Lorenzo. Do you have a car?"

"Yes."

"Would you give me a ride to Berkeley BART?"—the opposite direction, away from the freeway that we were practically on.

"Are you sure you're ready to leave?"

"After I take a shower, yes."

We both took showers. I sank into the jacuzzi, he went into the dry sauna.

A few minutes later, I ignored his "Hey!" and continued on to the urinal.

He rushed in behind me and told me: "If you're going to leave without me, just tell me, OK?"

"I'm going to give you a ride. I don't tell people I'm going to do something and then not do it. I'll pick you up at your locker."

"But you don't know where my locker is!"

"I know where the lockers are. I'll find you. Don't worry."

"You don't have to drive me, but if you aren't going to, just **tell** me, OK?"

"Relax! I'll meet you in a few minutes."

He was adjusting a black-and-white pullover workout top when I came up behind him and grabbed his ass. He jumped. I thought that he would have seen me coming—either from his peripheral vision my way or the other way in the mirror—but he hadn't. And he still didn't believe I would do anything other than zip out of the baths without him?

"You scared me!"

"How could you not see me coming?"

"I was concentrating on getting dressed." He pulled slinky black workout pants over his black cotton briefs. A nearly empty pack of cigarettes (Newports) fell to the floor.

Walking to the checkout desk, he said he wanted to smoke a cigarette before getting to the car. I told him to check out first, so that he could start on his cigarette. It also gave me a chance to hear his last name, which the attendants always ask for before giving the customer his valuables. The cigarette fell from his ear twice.

He did not go out and light up, but waited for me and went out with me. (Lest I go back to my room after he was gone?)

Walking to the car he asked if I went to the baths often.

"Most Thursdays, except the next four."

"Why's that?"

"Next Thursday is Christmas Eve, then I'm going to Bangkok."

"Wow! That's a long ways. You must have the bucks!"

"No, I have a husband who has free miles."

"What's that got to do with it?"

"He has miles for us both to fly free."

"Oh, **free** miles, I thought you said three miles. That didn't make any sense to me."

He did not comment on the not-inexpensive car. He approved of the music, which was old Temptations. He asked how I got into that kind of music. I said that I went to school in Michigan before Motown left Detroit, and Motown music was everywhere, and that my favorites were Smokey Robinson and Brenda Holloway

"Good music from way back."

"Yeah."

"I've heard that Michigan's a good school. Is it?"

"Yeah, in some things. It was a good school for me."

"I've never been back that way, but that's what I heard."

He told me that he worked nights doing maintenance in a community college. After asking my name, he told me that his was Gerald, but that he liked being called just "G."

"'G' for your g-spot' I couldn't find?"

He giggled. "Is **that** what you were trying to find!"

"Yeah, but I didn't find it."

"Yeah, well, it's not easy to make me cum."

"I noticed!"

"I liked what you did. You worked hard."

"Yeah."

"You like my ass, don't you?"

"Yeah."

He wrote down his full name and number, in case I ever wanted to call him, adding (a standard?) claim that he hardly ever goes to the baths, and seems to have to get a new membership every time he does go, because the card from the previous time has expired. He also claimed to have recently separated from a wife and to be trying to get another car. He thought I was being evasive about where I worked, when I told him my finances are complicated, and was also skeptical of my response to "You like to suck cock, don't you!" but was willing to accept that I liked sucking his cock.

He was startled that I thought he was kinky. "How do you know that?"

I didn't mention the questions about toys, but only that I had spent a long time suspended between his cock and his pussy. That satisfied him as an explanation (even if doing so had not made him cum).

He also told me that he had been eating too much junk food and too many meals at Denny's and asked if I would stop at a grocery store so that he could be some pork chops and potato salad to have a real meal. (He didn't mention any green, leafy vegetables.)

I told him that I had to get home, where my own dinner would be waiting for me (including some green, leafy vegetable). He pleaded some more, I reiterated that if I had time I would, but that I didn't have time.

However, I saw that coming back out University to the freeway would be impossible, because of a protest march, so when I turned on Shattuck, just before passing Berkeley BART, I asked him if he'd like a ride to Ashby BART instead. Once there, he asked me to take him to a "nearby" Safeway. We passed a freeway entrance, then MacArthur BART, and still further to a very large Safeway on Broadway. I was irritated. Why had I gone so far out of my way for him? He smokes. It's impossible to make him cum. He broke away from me four times before finally settling in with me. I guess it was that his open expression of what he wanted amused me.

He told me he would pay me to wait and drive him back to MacArthur BART. I was running very late and tried to impress on him that I was in a hurry. I didn't want money from him. What I didn't have was more time.

I went in and picked up a few items, then found him still in the meat department, trying to decide which package of pork chops to buy. Then he interrupted an employee talking to an elderly black woman for directions to potato salad.

Then he wanted "regular" potato salad, not "San Francisco style." I said that I had never heard of "San Francisco style" potato salad, that it looked "regular" to me.

We got in a checkout line, and suddenly he wanted potato chips, too. I told him, "If you're not back when my stuff gets checked out, I'm leaving."

"I'll be back, I'll be back. I just want to get some chips. I'll be right back." He hurried off.

I paid for my items and looked to see if I could see him returning. I couldn't. I told the checker, "I don't know what happened to this guy," and I left. G gave me a stiff back, a stiff neck, pulled away from me four times while I was servicing him, wheedled one thing as soon as I granted another, got me way out of my way and late. Enough!

I drove down to Grand and avoided the backup I would have encountered if I had gotten on the freeway at any of the exits north of the toll plazas. I felt bad about leaving G a long walk from a BART station, though he was closer both to San Lorenzo and to BART than when he started at the Steamworks. I felt that I had kept my promise to take him to BART and that he had broken his to be quick in Safeway (on top of lying about its closeness) and to get back before his stuff reached the checker.

Although I felt I had done more than I promised and chided myself for giving in to too many wheedlings, I regretted disappointing G. He had been so sure that I was going to leave him in the lurch, leave without him, and, eventually, I had.

The Regular

When I got to the Out Back, on another afternoon, there were no Greek gods visible on either level. The best-looking man in the pit, with dark hair, chiseled features, some belly, and a flaring rump was sucking the less-than-completely-hard dick of a white-haired man. I moved beside the man being sucked and peered down at the action, expecting that the cocksucker would want the more attractive man (me!). He glanced at me, but kept working where he was. The man being sucked reached over and caressed my chest. His hand slid down to feel my dick, which was standing at attention. He smiled at me and then leaned over and went down on me.

I thought that he should have been really happy that the most attractive candidate had chosen to suck his dick, and that he had continued after I provided an alternative. I don't at all understand why he would give up being sucked to try to service me, but he did. Worse for him, he wasn't good at it. He was hurting rather than pleasuring my dick, and very soon he was neither sucking nor being sucked. Only guilt kept me from withdrawing even sooner than I did.

About half an hour later, when I returned to the walkway around the cocksucker pit, there was a sizable black man in the pit waiting and watching. The hair on his head was closely cropped. The hair on his chest was thick and tightly curled. He had one of those famed bubble butts. He had some fat around the middle, but otherwise looked like a linebacker. A linebacker waiting to meet a rush?

He didn't retreat when I stood in front of him. I reached under my towel and gave my dick a few pulls. That was all the encouragement he needed to charge and swallow it. I rubbed his close-cropped scalp as he performed magic on my cock. His head felt familiar, though I couldn't recall where or when I'd felt it before.

I hung from a bar so that the center of my body arched toward him. I straightened up (so to speak!) to shoot in his mouth. He had been jerking off while sucking me and brought himself off as I was finishing. He flashed a grin up at me, and said, "That was great." I weakly agreed and thanked him. He grinned some more. I got dressed (glad to be sitting down) and left.

A few weeks later, I found the same heaven-sent black cocksucker again. This time, near rather than in the mosh pit. There is a bunk-bed, affording some privacy—not much, but some. That is, there is a wooden panel blocking the bed from the corridor, plus the ladder to the upper bunk. Lionel (I asked him his name later) knelt over me. Not having to hold myself up, I could swoon even more completely than when he sucked me off standing up a week before. I let him stick a finger up my asshole. Massaging his scalp I realized that this was the same man whose mouth I had been bequeathed by an older man months before. The hunk with the shaved head (then it was shaved, now his hair was short). This was the third, not the second time he was doing me.

The only way I could think of to delay cumming was to pull him up. His tongue completely fills my mouth. While avoiding gagging on his tongue cleaning my tonsils, I handled his cock—or part of his cock, which is more than a handful. I asked him if there were people (it would have to be men!) who could suck his dick. He smiled, and said "some."

I didn't try, and he gladly went back to doing all the work on both our cocks. I enjoyed massaging his scalp and also playing with his earlobes and nipples. These were large and loose. He moaned when I twisted his nipples, but otherwise concentrated on the two dicks. He wiped up the puddle of his own semen with his towel, and mock complained, "Now I need a new towel."

"I hope it was worth it," I commented.

"It was," he smiled. "I hope that I can see you again." This is when I asked, "Do you have a name,"

"Yeah, Lionel. Ever heard of anyone named that before?"

"My toy train, and Lionel Barrymore."

"Related to Drew?"

"Great uncle or something."

"How do you know him?"

"From 30s and 40s movies."

"I never heard of him before."

"And the son on 'The Jeffersons'."

"That's the one I was named for."

"I liked him."

"Yeah? I thought he was lame."

"He was pretty cute."

"Think so?"

"Yeah, but not as hot as you!"

This made him smile.

After exchanging his sticky towel for a fresh one, he got into the shower beside me. (The only one not beside me was occupied, so this did not signify much. As we were toweling off, I looked at his muscular thighs and jutting buttocks.

"You want to fuck me," he asked—neutrally, not at all leering.

"I want to, but there is no way I could cum again today."

"Maybe next time," he smiled. I patted his butt and slid my hand down his inner thigh. He kept smiling.

And when I kissed him, he grinned some more. I don't know how he understood it, but what I was saying, at least to myself, was "I don't just fuck your mouth in the dark, but kiss it in the light, where anyone can see."

On subsequent Thursday afternoon visits, Lionel found my cock, or I found his mouth—through gloryholes or in the mosh pit. Sometimes I waited for someone sucking his cock to stop before suggesting we go to my room. Lionel invariably turned up the dimmed light. He liked to look at me (my cock?). I liked to watch my cock going into his mouth. I admired the bulge of his thighs when he squatted in front of me. I enjoyed looking down and watching him stroking the impressive appendage that was his erect cock. I would play with it some, but mostly fondled (and sometimes sucked on) his nipples.

His dick was thick enough that I could choke on it even when it was limp. I asked if anyone could take it all when it was hard. "Up the ass, yeah, but hardly anyone can get it all in their mouth," he answered matter-of-factly.

He left large pools of semen behind: usually on the floor, but once on the sheets where he'd been kneeling as I stood on the bed, my back against the wall. Not in my mouth nor in the mouths of any of those who went down on him in the mosh pits while he was sucking my cock. He did not shoot easily, but he came copiously when finally he brought himself quietly off. No panting or other sound clues. He'd stop working his cock with his hands, but he'd also take breaks from "self abuse" while doing me, so I couldn't be sure from looking down and seeing no pistoning fist whether or not he'd cum.

He seemed grateful for any tit work and seemed to like being kissed in the mouth nearly as much as having his nipples licked and chewed. I knew that I could never suck him off (well, maybe if he was on the verge...in which case I'd be choked by the flood of cum). I was eager to find ways to give him pleasure, since I was receiving so much from him.

One week, the backroom with the mosh pit and gloryholes was closed, so that vending machines could be moved in and out. I'd planned to get a quick blowjob from someone, inhale some steam, and leave quickly, so I hadn't gotten a room. (A business with less contempt for its customers would have posted the information about an indefinitely extended closure of the steam room, but businesses selling men to men…)

I found the accretion of men in the video room comical. Other than the steam room and sauna where sexual activity was forbidden, and the rented rooms, which no doubt got more than usual amounts of action, the video room was the only place where sexual couplings could occur.

But they weren't. OK, I saw one blow job there, and several men playing with themselves, but it didn't turn into an orgy room as I expected it would. I guess it was too brightly lit (though still not very lit) and too public.

There was an open window from the main corridor. Either from it or from the flanking entryways, anything anyone did could be seen. So? What those in the mosh pit are doing to those above it is similarly visible to anyone who looks. I didn't understand the difference, and was willing to "perform" there if someone of interest would costar with me.

I was sort of watching a porn video when I felt someone looking at me through the window. I thought it might be Lionel, but, with the light behind him, I was only sure that it was a black man and that it was indeed me he was looking at. I took my cock out and played with it while holding his gaze for what seemed several minutes, but was probably less.

I was not surprised that after disappearing from the window, the man came in and smiled at me, or that it was Lionel. He said he didn't want to do anything there. I suggested he lean back against me while we waited for the outback to open. I'd have been happy to play with his tits and hold him, but he was restless.

A while later, I ran into him in front of the showers. We complained about the shutdown on a busy afternoon. (Why couldn't the transfer have been done during the slow morning hours?) I played with his tits and suggested we go back to the video room and get it on. He said, "I'm not an exhibitionist."

"I'm not either," I said, "but when there's no privacy available, I still like sex, and I want you bad."

He smiled noncommittally, and explained, "There are some people I'm trying to avoid."

By this time I was on the steps to the whirlpool, so that my crotch was at the level of his head. I fantasized about him sucking my cock through the railing. And thought of the number of times I had seen him sucking or being sucked and the number of times we had been visible to others while he sucked my cock, from the very first time on. I didn't mention either the fantasy or the memories, but he decided to wait no longer for a congenial (or at least familiar) space.

He motioned for me to follow him. Against a girder in the back corridor, he squatted, took out my cock, and began sucking it. The location was better lit than the video room and men stalking the corridors were bound to pass, and, given the lack of live shows, certain to stop and watch.

A black man who had earlier ignored me stopped to watch and started stroked himself under his towel. I pulled Lionel up, kissed him passionately, and went down on him. It was a political gesture on my part, a disavowal of the top's superiority. The voyeur moved closer, to a position in which I could have grasped or turned and sucked his cock. Neither of which I did. Lionel pulled me up and returned to fellating me.

The loudspeaker finally announced the reopening of the back room. "Let's go," I told Lionel.

We went to the darkest of the gloryhole cubicles. He crouched against the wall, so that my back was to anyone looking in or crowding in. I was perfectly willing to block, and am not sure who fondled various parts (tits and ass mostly) of me from behind.

At some point he told me that the men he had been trying to avoid were the very ones who found us in the hallway and hovered around watching us suck each other's cocks.

Not wanting to shoot yet, I went down on Lionel again, turning so that he could suck another cock through the gloryhole. When I got up to watch, Lionel returned to ministering to my rod. The man he'd been sucking moved away, but others peered over the top of the partition to watch Lionel going down on me.

After I shot on the floor, I sucked his cock some more. Then he sucked mine some more, and silently dropped a load on the floor. Since we were the first people back there, I'm fairly certain that the cum I slipped on was his, though I don't know why that should matter.

After steaming and showering I left.

The next week, I didn't think that the black man in that cubicle who sucked me off was Lionel, but it may have been. It didn't feel like him, but, in the near-dark, it is feeling his close-cropped skull that makes me certain I've found him, and I couldn't reach the head of the man who was ministering to my needs over the partition.

I was resting in my room when Lionel came by. I said hi and beckoned him in. As usual, he turned up the light. Unusually, I took his cock in my mouth first. I was still lying down, whereas he was standing.

We alternated, but I got the "I've already sucked you off" feeling from him—although "I feel like a top today" is a possibility. Whatever...

He came on my chest, while I was licking his balls and he was reaching back and diddling the approaches to his rear portal and he was doing the same to mine.

"Touching my asshole makes you cum?" I joked.

"No," I was hoping for a giggle, not a flat answer.

"Maybe it was my touching **your** asshole that made you come."

"No." Was there a trace of a smile? "Not any more." Does that count as volunteering information?

I asked him why he was trying to avoid certain people the week before. Did they know his lover?

He looked momentarily confused, then said, "No. It's that they follow me around and are always touching me."

"I can understand that. I like to touch you."

"But **you** I like to have touching me."

"Good," I smiled, not wanting to risk talking him out of that by rational analysis of their attributes or mine.

About every other week he did me. I always pulled him up to kiss, and generally paid token tribute to his excessive cock, sucking the head of it at least for a minute or so. Several times he laid beside me after we'd both cum. We cuddled and talked. When my cock began to stiffen again, he'd leave. I asked him why, but he just smiled.

Once he seemed particularly to be wiggling on my finger. I reached for lubricant and a condom and he continued to grind his hips backward as he watched me pick them up. I used two fingers to lubricate the path I planned to take. I still found the entryway narrow. Also, Lionel is 3–4 inches taller than I am, making thrusting up where the sun doesn't shine still more difficult. However, there was just enough room for him to lean on the bed and to bend his knees so that I could fuck him.

For once, there was an audible sigh when he ejaculated onto the floor, and perhaps I also felt his prostate contracting. I faked an orgasm (an advantage of condoms!) and kissed him while I removed the condom and wiped off my cock.

"I didn't think you liked to get fucked," I probed.

"I do. [Pause] Sometimes."

"Today?"

"Yeah. By you."

I was pleased with the more than minimal response and ventured to ask, "Does your lover fuck you?"

Lionel laughed. "No, never! I fuck him."

This surprised me. I thought he was a total bottom. "He can take it?"

He laughed again: "Oh yeah, he can take it all in one push."

I thought it would be impolite to comment on how loose the man's spookie must be to do that, but wanted to know more. "And he also can take your whole cock in his mouth?"

"Yeah, but he likes it better up the butt."

"Which do you like better?"

"I like to suck dick."

It was my turn to laugh. "I know **that**! I meant do you like to fuck or get sucked more?"

"Get sucked."

"How often does he do you?"

"Maybe once a month?"

"And how often do you fuck him?"

"A couple of times a week."

"How long have you been together?"

"Seven years."

"Seems pretty good for that long. [Pause] Does he come here, too?"

"No."

"Does he play around with other men?"

"No."

"Are you sure?"

"At least not when he's here—in town. When he travels, maybe."

"Do you like fucking him?"

"Yeah. It's OK."

"But not enough?"

"No. I need to suck dick, too."

"**Need** to?"

"Yeah. I've got to have it. I've been sucking dick since I was twelve."

"Who'd you suck when you were twelve?"

"A couple of guys."

"How old were they?"

"Thirteen, fourteen, fifteen."

"Which one taught you?"

"None of them. I always knew what to do, even the first time."

"How'd you know?"

"Probably I was born knowing what I wanted and how to do it."

"And you married a man you don't do."

"Right."

He didn't seem to feel anything contradictory about believing himself to be a natural-born cocksucker and to be coupled with a bottom.

"Are you having a seven-year itch?"

"Nah. We're solid."

"But you're here every other week."

"Yeah."

"Does he know?"

"No."

"Would he care if he knew?"

"He'd rather not know and I'm discreet."

"Promiscuous but discreet—"

"Right. I like dick—and so does he."

"But you don't go for it together—"

"You mean threesomes?"

"Or cruising together."

"No. He doesn't want to compete with me."

"And you want to compete with him?"

"Not especially. I satisfy him—"

"And satisfy yourself elsewhere."

"Yeah, you could say that."

I couldn't think of how to ask if his partner is black. Lionel has shown no interest in black men at the Steamworks. I've seen some white men sucking his cock, but I haven't seen him fuck anyone of any color. In other rooms? I don't know what happens there. But he's said he prefers being sucked to fucking, so…Before I completed this chain of inferences, he actually volunteered information by continuing, "I don't fuck anyone except him, and I only get fucked once or twice a year."

"But you like it?"

"Yeah, you **know** I like it. I used to more."

"Like it more or get fucked more often?"

"Both."

"What happened?"

"I got older. I settled down. Or something. And you, do you like to fuck?"

"I like to fuck you!"

He chortled. "But not in general."

"I've never fucked a general, that I know of."

"You **know** what I meant!"

"I don't like to fuck in general, only in particular. I didn't used to have to wonder if I'd be hard enough to do it, but now my dick's unreliable."

"Far as I can tell, it's hard most of the time."

"Not really. It used to be."

"Too bad I didn't know you then."

"Well, then, I shot fast, and you don't like to stick around for a second helping."

Noncommittal: "Mmmmm. I like to see who you'll get to relieve you after me."

"I don't do as well."

"That's **good**! Keeps you comin' back for more."

"And if you did me twice in a day, you don't think I would?"

"No. Usually when I cum, I want to leave,"

"But sometimes I see you again, later, prowling the back."

"Sometimes I just look around."

"How much can you see in a dark cubicle with you mouth full?"

This provoked something between a snort and a chuckle. "I can't, but usually I just look around and leave."

"But sometimes you find something irresistible—"

"Yeah, something like that."

Two weeks later, after he's sucked me off and jacked himself off, I veered back to his early experiences (and repetition).

"You told me you've been sucking cock since you were twelve."

"Yeah?"

"And you started with some older boys."

"Yeah, brothers."

"Together?"

"At the same time? No. One after the other."

"And the other two would watch you do their brother, their brothers?"

"Yeah. I'd do the oldest, then the next oldest, then the youngest."

"And the oldest wasn't ready again when you finished?"

"Sometimes. The youngest shot real fast, but the middle one took a long time."

"What about you?"

"At first, I couldn't shoot, but I played with my dick while I did each of them."

"And then?"

"One day I shot."

"Doing which one?"

"The oldest."

"And you went on and did his brothers after you came?"

"Yeah. I didn't like it as much. Once I learned how to know when I was about to get off, and could control it, I made sure not to shoot too soon."

"So you'd hold back until you were sucking the youngest one?"

"Yeah."

"None of them wanted to fuck you while you sucked one of his brothers?"

"I don't know. Maybe, but they didn't try. They were used to waiting their turn."

"You didn't try doing two of them at the same time?"

"They were not small—and I didn't know it was possible."

"Now?"

"Now I know it's possible, but it's awkward and you can't get either one in very far."

The conversation moved on to Maui, where he was going the next week. Although I know nothing of gay life there, I could at least run through the major sites. It would be hard to miss Haleakala, of course.

Three weeks later I learned Lionel had had a good time on Maui and played Lucky Pierre with his lover and an Angeleño. So his lover knew he was fuckable, at least on occasion. For me, the occasion did not recur, though I lured him to my room many more times and we kissed and talked (and he sucked my cock and jacked himself off).

I gave him my phone number and suggested that if he was in The City any weekday afternoon to visit, but he was too fearful of being caught by my lover. He's never given me his phone number (home or work) or address. We continue to connect periodically and have friendly and good sex.

The Fan

The next black man I met at the Steamworks was Kevin Beaumont. Beaux monts would have fit, but they were under him and obscured by steam when we made first contact with each other.

The steam room was unusually full. A fairly large (say 6' 210–220 pound.) black man told me there was space beside him. I crawled up to sit beside him. I placed my leg very close to his, but not quite touching it. He closed the distance almost immediately.

I couldn't see well, but I saw that, in his lap, a large firehose was stiffening. I reached over to play with it. Even fully erect, the head of his penis remained sheathed. I slid the foreskin back and forth while he moaned softly. What I thought was left-over cum was precum (he later told me).

After a few minutes of jacking him off, I asked him if he'd like to come to my room. In the showers he looked more brown than black. His body was muscular and hairy. He was balding, and had a thick mustache.

In my room my tongue explored under the foreskin. I also chewed on it (gently), and took as much of his cock into my mouth as I could manage. Some loose foreskin tickled my throat and I nearly gagged. I supplemented my oral ministrations with vigorous handwork. (Is it handiwork?).

I was on my knees and Kevin bent over to caress my buttocks. "You've got a really fine ass," he cooed.

I didn't respond, but continued to use my mouth.

He warned me he was about to cum (in case I didn't want him to ejaculate in my mouth). His load was thick and salty—and considerable. I spit out the liquid and took back the solid. It was almost as large as it had been when it was erect, though there was now nearly two inches of foreskin bunched over nothing in particular.

"I've never met anyone with so much foreskin," I told him.

"I could tell you liked it."

"Mmm-hmmm."

"Recalling farther back, he said, "I didn't think I'd ever get your attention."

"Really? When you invited me to sit beside you—"

"There really wasn't any other place you could have sat."

"I was hoping it was an invitation."

"Well, that, too. But earlier I was looking at you."

"Where?"

"You were on the exercise bicycle. Your towel kept slipping off and I was watching every time it did. And I was watching your legs pump the pedals and wishing I was the bicycle seat."

"Oh?!"

"I was on the treadmill and I forced myself to go faster."

"To show me your endurance?"

"Something like that. Or just from the excitement of watching you."

"You could have said something!"

"I didn't have any indication that you were interested. I thought you just wanted to work out."

"I wasn't thinking of sex. Trying to keep my towel up and get some exercise was all I could think of."

"Well, after I finished my workout, I went to the steam room and thought I was going to go home without doing anything else. I didn't expect that you'd come in and sit beside me—"

"And grope you?"

"I knew from how you sat close to me that you were interested."

"I couldn't see much. Well 'much' is what I saw between your legs, and I was intrigued by your foreskin."

"I should remember to thank my momma for not snipping it off."

"Yeah, do that. And thank her for me, too."

He laughed and said, "I'm not sure that would be a good idea."

"She doesn't know you're gay?" (Are you gay?)

"She knows that, but don't want to think about who be doing what to who."

After establishing that we both lived in The City and talking about or places of origins (New Orleans in his case), we showered again.

From his locker he extracted black bikini briefs and tucked his thing down. I asked if it didn't hurt for him to sit down. He asked what I meant.

"To sit on your cock."

"I don't sit on it. It's not that big."

"But it's tucked between your legs in your underwear. Doesn't it get crushed when you sit down."

He laughed, "No. If it did, I'd have to store it somewhere else."

I was skeptical, but he was the expert on how he sat, right? I watched him add black jeans and a red -and-black flannel shirt, topped by a 49er warm-up jacket and 49er cap (which he wore with the bill forward).

"Oh, you're a 49er fan?"

"Most definitely. Five Super Bowls. I've watched very game since 1981."

"Except for some taping problems, I have, too."

"Go Nick! Go Niners!"

"Rah, rah!"

At the checkout counter, Kevin wrote down addresses and phone numbers. I kissed him good-bye and he left.

After a few 49er-game-discussion e-mails, he made a house-call one afternoon. We undressed each other in my bedroom.

I donned his 49er cap, bill-backward. He sat on the bed reaching over me to play with my ass, which he again remarked was "very fine." He asked if I ever got fucked. I said no and that he was so big that he would tear me apart. He assured me that he could be very gentle and patient.

"I'm sure you could, but I don't do that."

As I was panting, doing us both, he began urging me to "give it up." Not my ass to penetration, the usual meaning, but my load. I obeyed, splattering the towel I was kneeling on.

As soon as I was done, he followed me over the edge, with plentiful moans and encouragements. I swallowed this time, and the next.

What was different about the next time was that he got me up on the bed and we 69ed. He was looking at and fingering my backdoor, murmuring, "I'd sure like some of that!"—A complete reversal from the days of my youth for me to suck and not get fucked…

Was it being dropped after "giving it up" to Raju that inhibited me? Kevin had a lot to drive with and I knew it would hurt going in (and that I'd then start to enjoy it). He was polite and personable and there was his mesmerizing fore-skin———which would be lost/wasted up my ass. I wanted to play with it, chew it, lick inside it, not have it buried deep inside my rear end.

Eventually, back on my knees, with more verbal encouragement ("give me that juice, cum for daddy," etc.), I brought myself off. He again followed nearly immediately. (Such control! Why don't I have it?) He may have wanted me to bend over, but what his presence did was make me want to get on my knees and lick and chew his foreskin.

He said that he was glad that I was home when we made dates and complained that other men even didn't show up for dinner dates. He was starting to expect to be stood up. I guess that not everyone was as mesmerized by his epic foreskin as I was, but they seemed very silly to me, as well as rude.

I saw him again on the treadmill at the baths. I told him my room number and invited him to pay me a visit. I think it was the day that I fucked Lionel, and I was doing that and ignored a knock on my door. I'd have liked to add Kevin to make a threesome, but didn't want to offend Lionel. I thought that he might not want anyone—especially anyone black?—joining us and/or seeing that he was getting fucked.

Kevin came back later and commented that I seemed to be having a good time when he was by earlier. I agreed and told him that I'd thought about opening the door and inviting him to join us.

"What was you doing?"

"Fucking."

"Hmmm. I didn't know you fucked."

"Just don't get fucked." Reiterate that and move on! I wasn't ready to cum again, but played with myself some while bringing Kevin off."

"We should get together in The City some time soon," was his parting shot. But he didn't respond to an invitation to watch the 49ers a weekend I was alone or to e-mail suggestions of a couple of other possible rendez-vous times.

That's what happens when one finds out what they like and how they like it and don't give it to them just that way, I guess. In the olden days, there was the instance of frustration that I wouldn't suck (though I offered my ass as a substitute), now that I wouldn't get fucked (though I offered my mouth as a substitute).

Or, "it's so easy to leave me/alone with my memories." Writing them down keeps them clearer, even if it can't make them live again.

"Always and forever"

A large black man was in the darkest gloryhole cubicle. Size and color were all I could see, but I soon also learned that he gave very good head. So I invited him to my room, where I could lie back and be pleasured.

I noticed that he kept his towel on as he knelt over me. After a while, I loosened it with my feet and it dropped off. He never touched himself. There was something, though nothing very substantial in front. It occurred to me that he had been a she, that is, that this was a female-to-male transsexual. Given the quality of head, I didn't care.

To my warning that I was going to cum, he only murmured. After he'd drained me, he refastened his towel, sat up, and told me "I love cum. I love sucking cock." I felt that was less than personal praise, but there are other satisfactions and I was very satisfied.

Asking if he could see me again was more personal. So was asking if I was married.

"All the good ones are married" didn't seem very personal either, although clearly intended as a compliment. "But I can still give you what you want on the side, and you'll be wanting it again."

"That's a safe bet," I admitted. "That kind of pleasure can easily be addictive."

He smiled smugly.

The name he wrote was "Gerard" with a Berkeley flatland address and phone number.

I called him early the next week and he invited me to come over the next morning around 10. The apartment seemed very 1970s with macramé plant-holders, shag carpets, and some museum posters from that era. There were two aquariums and the heat was on. No books or magazines. A large tv screen to which two video-recorders were attached. On top of the tv were framed pictures of a boy and a girl, both darker than Gerard.

Gerard bathed my balls with his tongue and deep-throated my cock. Why wouldn't I "cum good"?

Before I left home, I'd taken Viagra and, buoyed by it, after I went to piss, I noticed there was new life in it—just as in the olden days. Gerard had put on a robe and was on his couch watching Ed Koch carry on as a crusty judge.

"How can you be hard again?" Gerard asked.

"Hoping to attract your interest" (and hoping to distract it from the tv).

"You have, you have. Come over here and let me take care of it."

I stood between him and the tv. Even facing away from it, I was not able to ignore it altogether and followed the case even as I was being serviced. I was as impressed by his stamina as he was by my resiliency...

After swallowing a second, lighter load, he said he needed to get ready for work and asked if I wanted to drink some tea with him. I didn't want any caffeine, but he had chamomile. Mid-day seemed early for it, but I'm flexible. (Even to tolerating the continuing drone of some talk show on tv.)

Gerard emitted a bunch of rhetoric about wanting to feed me and take care of me in every way that discouraged me from giving him my phone number.

He told me that he was going with some coworkers to Reno that weekend. He'd never been there. I warned him that it would be cold. Although he had grown up in northern Florida, he was familiar with snow and real winter from having been stationed in Connecticut and Korea in the military. (He didn't specify a service, but Connecticut seems to indicate navy.) He re-enlisted once, but didn't continue, moving to Detroit with a man he'd met and fell in love with in Korea. I wondered if that was the father of his children when he was a woman, but couldn't think of any way to ask if he'd borne children. His hips were certainly wide enough. And he'd kept his undershorts on in bed, just as he'd kept the towel on at the bathhouse. If my guess was right, Gerard was not eager to tell me that he was christened Geraldine (or some other female name). If I was right, it was not going to change anything, but I couldn't think of a tactful way to ask. Our very own "don't ask, don't tell" policy was in effect.

On the phone, he told me he had a great time in Reno, wanted to go back, and now wanted to visit Las Vegas. I asked if he serviced his coworkers. He said they worked for him and he wouldn't be able to manage them if he sucked their cocks. But he was eager to suck mine.

I was happy to oblige. And to be obliged. He rimmed me thoroughly before extracting my first load.

There was a closed door between the bathroom and his bedroom. I opened it (heedless of the fate of Bluebeard's wives...). There was a child bicycle and two bunk beds. No decoration, no clutter: it was very institutional-looking.

I returned to his bed and received some more pleasuring. I asked him to remove his jockey shorts. He said, "You've seen it," which was only vaguely true. Nonetheless, he complied. Was it surgically constructed? Was it functional? All I was sure of is that it wasn't hard.

After expelling my second load and taking a shower, I had chamomile tea again, with some soap opera blaring from the tv. I was put off by the blare and by the content. Gerard again laid out a line of services he'd like to perform for me. I could not imagine myself living with someone who watched 8–10 hours of tv a day, especially daytime soap operas and romance-channel movies. Other than his very able sucking of my cock, we had nothing in common. He was considerate and hard-working and, I decided, too domestic to be an FTM. Not very hung and impotent and abashed, or even modest(?!), not a transsexual.

A few days later, we had another 10 a.m. date. I knocked. No response. The television was off, so he had to be gone. I sat outside about 20 minutes, then went to have coffee. An hour later, still no one was there. I left a note and stopped back again around 4. This time there was music from inside. I saw the girl from the picture and decided I didn't want to scare her. If she was home alone, surely she had been taught not to open the door to men she didn't know.

As I was walking away, she came out, told me Gerard was at work, and asked if she could give him a message.

I told her to tell him that Nick had stopped by.

After that, I only got the answering machine. The first time, I left a message (with my phone number) asking why he'd stood me up. I left a few more messages telling him who was calling. I did not mention all his talk about taking care of me, sexually and in any other way I'd let him.

Was it crossing his daughter's path that freaked him out? Embarrassment at standing me up? Finding Mr. Righter? It irritates me not to know. Almost enough (having written this) to make another unscheduled stop to try to ask him.

Blatino non-explosion

Rather than end on that sour note, I want to end with Rafael. But, first, another brief encounter that I remember fondly

Having been sucked off (skillfully) by a balding white man, I was in the mosh pit, seeking visual stimulation, but with my other senses open. A lean black man wearing a glisteningly white jockstrap caught my eye. His smooth, long legs were muscular, but not in a bulging way (though his calves were rounded). The sides of his head were shaved. He had a smooth chest, with large (in diameter) nipples. And the prototypical washboard abdomen. Thick eyebrows close to his wide eyes, curving upward on the outsides. Large ears with sideburns half their length, hair cut short. He had a not particularly thick mustache, and a thick pubic forest extending above his jockstrap.

My appreciative examination of his crotch drew him over so that he was standing over/in front of me. I felt what seemed a manageable appendage. I have generally found the adage about black male penises "What you see is what you get" accurate. Most thicken when they harden but do not lengthen appreciably. Removing this one from its pouch, I didn't know that it was an exception to the rule. I was met by a smile and a slight stirring in what I was holding. I licked the head. Its length increased at least two inches and it defied gravity to rise above parallel to the floor.

I played with his balls, played with his tits, ignored my own born-again hard-on, and failed to make him cum. My jaw was tiring when he suggested a break. I readily agreed (insofar as it was a suggestion rather than a euphemism for withdrawing). I liked his big eyes and friendly smile, as he thanked me.

Perhaps half an hour later, I was in the same situation again. That is, I had shot another load and was back watching such action as there was from the pit. A difference was that I now knew how big the man's dick was. He had traded his jockstrap for a towel and was semi-hard when we moved to reunite my mouth and his probe. It had been a break rather than the end after all!

As soon as I resumed sword-swallowing, another (leaner, younger) white man started pulling on the thigh of the man I was fellated, trying to pull him away from my mouth. Even knowing that I had more than I could manage (had bitten off more than I could chew?), I was pleased by the loyalty (that is, what I interpreted as loyalty; it may have had any number of other motivations). My competitor crouched down so that his mouth was at the same level as my head and the black man's dick. He continued to try to turn the black man toward him, and continued to be resisted.

I had rationalized that the interloper could probably take more and do better than I could. But I continued, leaving it to the possessor of the long hard cock to decide into whose mouth he wanted to put it. During this contest, I had looked up a number of times to see if I was going to be supplanted. When he caught my eye, the black man smiled at me. I also saw him squint hostilely at my rival. I won the contest. The dubious reward for me was having more work to do. I don't think the reward for him was a great blow-job. I hope it was at least a satisfactory one. Plus the exercise of choice on his part.

Still not having cum, he thanked me when I tired and told me he had enjoyed my attentions.

If I saw him again, I would probably resume my efforts. Not just in gratitude: I consider him very attractive, physically and from what little I've surmised or imagined of his character.

And onto Rafael: more surprises.

I think that he was returning to cruise my room when I nearly ran into him leaving it. I made a circuit. When I completed it, he was standing at the end of the aisle. I kept my eyes on him as I passed and then paused, looking back, from my doorway.

Presently, he followed, asking from the hall "How's it going?"

"It would be better if you came in."

"I was hoping for an invitation," he said, smiling, and closing the door behind him.

"I thought I gave you a lot of invitation on the way back. I'm glad you waited for me to make a circuit."

"A what?"

"To go around and come back to where you were."

"Ah, a circuit, yeah. I hate this music."

"Me, too. Probably it encourages people to leave faster."

"It does me, though we've both been here quite a while."

"Oh? How do you know?"

"I have a room across the hall and down two doors."

I remembered that I'd been intimidated by the size of the dick on a man I had not realized was this one. Other than that and my general unease about interpreting interest from someone sitting motionless and expressionless in a cubicle, I had been attracted to him. Having invited him into my room, I had to try to provide him some pleasure.

It was not unpleasant for me. It helped that the head of his cock was relatively small and hooded. I couldn't take his whole cock in my mouth, but he seemed to like what I was doing with the outmost third of it. I explored his spookie with first one and then two fingers. It was not loose, but it was not clamped shut either. I shifted positions several times, but finally gave up.

"You've earned a rest," he agreed. "It's my turn to do some work."

I was pleasantly surprised. Having often gone down on men whom I wanted to fuck and pried open their closed rear entrances, I was amused to have someone trying that on me.

"Don't even think about it," I exclaimed.

"I can't help thinking about it." He flashed a smile. More seriously, he asked, "You don't ever get fucked?"

"No."

"Never?"

"Not for many years."

"Why not?"

"I was sort of raped once." I don't know why I pulled that from the deep-freeze of my memory. Perhaps terror at the inordinate size of what Rafael wanted to put into me.

"Mmmm. By someone like me?"

"No. You're much nicer." If the question was about race, I ignored it.

"I'm goooood."

"Probably, but you're way too big, even if I did get fucked."

"Nah. I'm gentle and patient."

"But we're **not** going there."

"A man can try."

"Sure. And, if at first you don't succeed, and try again, sometimes you still don't succeed. Anyway, if I was into fucking, it would be better for me to fuck you."

He cocked one eyebrow. "Why is that?"

"My dick isn't so gigantic, and I think you are also not as tight." I realized the latter part could be taken as an insult, though I was ready to rush in to stress that I was only making a comparison, not saying he wasn't tight.

He responded instead to the first part: "Your cock isn't at all small. It may not be as long as mine, but it's thicker." At least the head is.

Only after this impasse did I learn that his name was Rafael. When I asked what his name was, he replied "Ralph." I said: "Is that short for Rafael or am I wrong that you are Latino."

"No. I'm Latino alright, from Puerto Rico originally. I tell people 'Ralph' because I am afraid they'll call me 'Rafel.'"

"Yeah, that **is** an abomination. And I don't understand how it happened. The name in English is three syllables—Raphael. Even if people growl the a's wrong, there's no reason not to pronounce the middle syllable."

"But Americans don't need to be reasonable, especially when it comes to Spanish names."

"Well, they generally get the 'Jolla' right in 'La Jolla' and the 'José' in "San José.' Although the a's are almost always wrong."

"You pronounce the names in Spanish? Always?"

"Almost always. I was once totally puzzled by someone asking me where 'valley joe" street was, and I was on Green Street, only a block away from Vallejo [vah-yay-ho]. "Rafael laughed. "I almost always say Los Angeles, and usually San Francisco [with Spanish a's, accents on the penultimate syllables, and something appropriately close to 'hell' in 'Angeles'].

"Do you speak Spanish?"

"Only a little."

"Where did you learn it?"

"In Mexico."

"In school there?"

"For all of three weeks."

"In Cuernavaca?"

I laughed. "Less grand than that, in Uruapan."

"Where's that?"

"In Western Mexico, Michoacán."

"Like the *paletas*?"

"Yeah. They have great *paletas* there, but also everywhere else in Mexico, too."

"Even Tijuana?"

"Maybe, though I don't consider Tijuana really Mexico."

"And Puerto Rico?"

"I definitely don't consider Puerto Rico part of Mexico."

Rafael guffawed. "No, I mean do you consider it part of America."

"Owned by America. And you?"

"I have some uncles who want it to be independent, but so much money flows that way, it would be stupid to cut off the flow. But I don't much care."

"It should be up to the people who live there."

"Exactly!"

"When did you leave?"

"When I was four."

"Where did you grow up?"

"Los Angeles" [Spanish pronunciation].

"There aren't many puertoriceños there, are there?"

"There's a lot of everything there. Some PRs."

"And where do you live now?"

"In Berkeley, within walking distance of here."

"Wow! I hardly ever meet anyone here who is actually from Berkeley. It's like finding a native-born white San Franciscan!"

I told him the places in Berkeley I had lived. Having discussed "What do you do?" in the sexual sense, we did not get into the occupational sense. I needed to leave and thanked him for not waiting any longer than he had to make my acquaintance.

He said that he hoped to see me again, and I reciprocated. I do hope to meet him again and perhaps expand the sexual repertoire of our first encounter. This was only last week, so who knows?

Conclusions

Before reading my accounts of my relatively recent sexual encounters with black men, I thought that I had just picked up where I left off sixteen years earlier, when I withdrew from "the hunt." Although my position(s: older, married, HIV+) have changed, I feel that I am the same person, attracted to the same kinds of men I was attracted to when I was twenty-something. This could mean I have learned nothing, which may be true. However, I think I am a little more relaxed about rejection and a bit more accommodating, though my long-ago self strikes me as already having been overeager to please. (Maybe he was just trying out various roles, however.)

It is clear to me that there are continuities between my late-twenties and late-forties. In particular, I still respond to desire. I continue to be attracted to those who give evidence of being attracted to me. I have a "type"—well, several "types"—but my contacts are not confined to any one "my type." What I wrote about the encounters in Book I applies to those in Book II as well:

> I wanted to be wanted, and was willing to adapt to the sexual scenarios of those who wanted me. I did not require appearances of love or even the possibility of love developing from the sex. What mattered was being desired by a man, not any particular attributes.

Similarly, I remain sexually versatile, albeit much more oral and less anal than I was in the era before AIDS. It is not that I fear being infected with another strain of HIV (if being fucked) or condom failure infecting someone else (someone I'm fucking). Rather, there is so much outbound traffic through my back chute every day that I am reluctant to allow two-way traffic. (I'm especially concerned about head-on collisions in the dark tunnel!). As for fucking, my dick is not dependable enough, the frustrations and mortifications of failure are too acute to risk. A semi-hard dick can be blown, but can't push up through a tight sphincter.

I always liked to have my cock sucked—always, that is, as long as it wasn't being scraped. My ability to ingest cock has increased—some. My stamina has also increased some. What has changed dramatically, is my interest in it. In days of old, it was occasional, unpleasant duty. Now it is a form of pleasure. To my astonishment, these days, my dick more reliably rises when I'm sucking than when I'm being fucked, or trying to fuck.

How can that be? Because sex is more in the mind than in the body? Hmmmm. Perhaps it is that I am choosier about whom I suck than I am about whom I let go down on me? (On Thursday afternoons) I let most anyone who does not repulse me put my dick in his mouth. How long it stays there depends on the quality of servicing it's receiving.

In contrast, unless I'm very bored, I only go down on men I find attractive. This is not such a small set. Although I admire svelteness, it is not a major criterion. Those to whom I offer my mouth must be at least as dark as I am. This eliminates about half the white men. Among those of all three races who are darker than I am, I have no particular preferences for skin shade. I don't believe "The darker the berry, the sweeter the juice;" at least it does not apply to cum. I have never found cum that was sweet (and probably would be alarmed if I did!). Variances in sourness and saltiness do not seem at all related to skin coloration. Perhaps more experienced cocksuckers can tell how much cum of what quality is in the sacs they inspect, but I can't. Besides, I rarely swallow it and often do not even taste it.

Among those qualifying on the darker-than-me criterion, a smile goes a long way, though so does a look of lust. Very few men smile while they are on the sexual hunt. I doubt that I do, at least I doubt that I smile first. I may reflect one back.

Beyond looking at me with friendliness and/or desire, and not being too white, at least my prime conscious criterion is meaty thighs and butts. Not that I seek to thrust my dick between their thighs or up their butts, only that I enjoy running my hands over the dark orbs and up and down the columns, while my mouth works on their rods. I prefer smooth thighs, but find many hairy ones exciting, too. Firmness, not ground cover is what excites me.

I am an inverted size queen—or is it being a reverse size queen? Not only do I prefer small, but I prefer them limp (but erectable). I enjoy feeling a cock swell in response to what I'm doing. I have not failed to notice that I found the dicks of six of the eight men I've written about in Book II (and more in Book I) uncomfortably oversized for my petit, tooth-filled mouth to accommodate. I don't think this means I am deluded about what I like or lying. (Yeah, I've heard the claim, "There are two kinds of gay men: size queens and liars.") Remember that this is my black book! I find most black dicks excessive. In the same span of time, I'm sure I sucked the cocks of five Asians or Pacific Islanders and two or three white men (including Latinos) for each black one. At most, ten percent of these non-black ones were too big for me. I find black men attractive **despite** their usual cock size, not because of it. (And don't try to convince me that black men, at least black gay men, are not bigger! The size ranges by race overlap, and there are a few Asian/Pacific Islander ones bigger than some black ones, but the averages are definitely **not** the same. I doubt this is only true for men who have sex with men, though they are whom I've observed and compared.)

I'm a leg man, not a tit man. I play with nipples when it seems to please their owner, but the size and texture of chests is not important to me. I don't like fat, my own or anyone else's, but bellies do not stop me or turn me off. I thought Jabba's would block access and found it revolting, but what was below it asserted its charms (and/or his grossness stimulated the pleasures of abjection?).

I value politeness and consideration, though it is very difficult to guess whether these are going to be evidenced when initial contact is made in wordless semi-darkness. I like to cuddle and to converse (Raju, Lionel, Kevin, Rafael) not to fly apart as soon as climax is achieved.

In comparison to my younger self, I am now much less concerned that the sex be reciprocal. The sexual roles (top/bottom) in none of these relationships approached equivalency in frequency or duration. Still, tops Raju, Kevin, and Rafael all also went down on me; Jabba, the unnamed horizontal-man and even to some extent G took some consideration of my comfort. No longer expecting reciprocity, I still appreciate concern for my pleasure, as I at least try to consider the discomforts and pleasures of those doing me (like Lionel; Gerard deflected the interest in his dick that I showed).I enjoyed Rafael and Kevin urging me on while I was servicing them. I was right to distrust the lines Gerard (and G) laid on me. There was minimal exchange of words between me and either of the men with whom my only connection was in the mosh pit (both thanked me, and I am not faulting their politeness). This leaves only Lionel as the only African American one not sweet-talking me (along with the South Asian Raju, who had his own expressive style).

As before, some of the men were taking the opposite role "in public" that they took with their lovers. Lionel and Raju were exclusively tops at home, interested in being topped by me. In retrospect, I suspect that Rafael was a bottom at home and a top "abroad." G and Kevin did not have partners. I'm relatively sure that Kevin was predominantly a top. G's focus of pleasure was lower than the cock he offered to many men (offers more than a few took up). Perhaps his ex-wife had tired of playing with his booty or plugging his ass with dildoes? Gerard was a total bottom. With this last exception it seems to me that there was less strict role maintenance than was the case with my earlier black partners. (I don't know if this is a function of changes in my aura, changes in the social world over time, or is an accident of my "sample" of partners. I don't think that those in Book II are notably older than were those in Book I, so that "maturation" does not seem likely an explanation to me.) Nonetheless, there still seemed to be some of the same switching from whatever the usual sexual role at home (with the man's lover) was.

I did not pick up any of the dreaded equation of sexual receptivity with femininity. None of those I serviced called me "bitch", "punk", etc. I remain somewhat uneasy about the possibility.

Life partner is an office that is already permanently occupied. I was not auditioning possible replacements. I was seeking a dependable regular sex partner as well as the excitement of novelty and hunting. I'd have liked Raju to take me as a regular concubine or to have taken Lionel as one. I was exploring whether great sex was enough to sustain an ongoing relationship with Gerard when he cut off communications. I'm ready to try to build a sexual friendship with Rafael (though we didn't exchange numbers) and even thought of seeing G again (before abandoning him in an Oakland Safeway, or before he abandoned me in an Oakland Safeway checkout line after repeated warnings from me). None provided a regular, reliable connection that would remove me from the scene where we met.[1] This is not that I don't want an association with the kind of person who goes to the baths. I am well aware that I am that kind of person!

The *frisson* of cultural differences often gives me pleasure. Not just an erotic charge, but the ongoing excitement of learning about other ways of being in the world: individual as well as cultural. The availability of such explorations is one of the glories of the Bay Area.

What of class? The great American unmentionable, since "everyone here is middle class"? I don't think that everyone in gay bathhouses is middle class. With clothes checked and the uniform of a white towel, wordless encounters contain few class markers. Hair-styling and body tone may have some relationship to class

---

1.   I could say with Samuel Delany, "Most [of our sexual encounters] were affable but brief because, beyond pleasure, these were people you had little in common with. Yet what greater field and force than pleasure can human beings share?" (*Times Square Red, Times Square Blue*, p. 56). However, I didn't always find out whether we had anything in common (nor did he).

status, but are unreliable markers, because some affluent men don't care about stylish coiffures or go to the gym and some working-class men have stylish haircuts and well-toned bodies (some gym-toned, some work-toned). How someone talks (along with the content of some talk) is more reliable. Sometimes literally "tell-tale"!

I suspect that Raju derives from an elite family, but I'm not certain of that. His "class origins" and current position both seem to me above mine. Despite speaking standard English (though often in unusual ways), G clearly was working class. I didn't experience my relationships with Lionel, Kevin, Gerard, or Rafael as interclass. Probably our grand-parents and great-grandparents were American peasants, some of their great-great-grandparents slaves (while mine were European peasants). So far as I could tell—which was not very far—they had middle-class jobs.

If there were class differences, I did not eroticize theme. Only G seemed to find me exotically different in class. And even he did not emit any particular signals of feeling that he was mastering the usual master/oppressor class, or even the managerial one. Since there was no one to force me to do what I did with him/for him/to him, he seemed to suppose that I enjoyed what I did with him. (To some extent I did, though I was annoyed by his flitting away, by his questions, and by the impossibility of making him cum.)

As for exploitation, perhaps I am blind, but I don't see it herein. I don't feel that all interracial contact inevitably involves exploitation, or that unreciprocal sex necessarily evidences a master-slave dialectic. I suppose one could say that everyone at a gay bathhouse is exploiting the desires of potential partners—and the desire for potential partners.

Readers will reach their own conclusions about equity and exploitation, but I feel that in the only near instance of exploitation, it was G who somewhat exploited me. I don't mean by lack of sexual reciprocity. In that I voluntarily continued, I presumably appeared to him to be enjoying what I was doing, focused as it was on getting him off. I liked what I did sexually with the other men and have reasons to suppose they liked what they did, whether they were tops or bottoms with me. How much patience did I owe G because he was poorer and less mobile? Who was patient both as he flitted from mouth to mouth in the baths and in driving out of the way and offering to drive him again if he returned to the groceries he had accumulated? That's my brief for the defense, anyway!

Obviously, I had resources G lacked, notably access to a car. In the bathhouse, I had a room, which costs more than a locker ($20+ and $12, respectively). Every one in the Steamworks has paid for entry and the eight-dollar difference looms larger for some than for others. One cannot, however, presume that those in the Out-Back don't have rooms. I am far from being the only one lacking the patience and passivity to wait in my room for someone to venture inside! Moreover, the decision about whether to rent a room often depends on how much time the man can stay (and availability: there is often a waiting list). Those who can only stay an hour or two mostly take lockers. And there is reason to suppose that those with little time have more financial resources. This is because it is those with careers and those in relationships who show up for (relatively) short durations of time on a weekday at a gay bathhouse. There is no neat calculus of working class men getting lockers while middle- or upper-class men get rooms. Raju, the most clearly affluent of these men, did not have a room either of the times I saw him at the Steamworks.

If I only sexually connect with men darker than I am, it is difficult to argue that I don't eroticize racial differences. I am not convinced that I do, because I find attractive "Caucasians" and "my type" (Latino) is nominally of the same race, though most have some Native American (*indigeno*) blood.

Indubitably, there are black racial characteristics that excite me (lip thickness, thigh smoothness, and butt jut), as well as at least one that repels me (cock size), and others that I appreciate but don't seek or require. I respond to men with a wide range of hair textures, extents of body hair, of head hair, and of facial hair.

Sweat? Yes, I do. Abundantly. Some of my sexual partners do, too (Lionel and Kevin, in particular). In the bathhouse, most customers shower multiple times. The black men I met there and have seen elsewhere (Gerard, Kevin, G, and I could add Raju) have been fastidiously clean and freshly showered. Sweat is another neutral attribute for me, neither a turn-on nor a turn-off.

Although I do not think it is true, I feel somewhat vulnerable to the charge recurrently leveled against white men who have only sexual relationships with black men, that is, "You like to fuck with us when you're horny, but don't want to live with us on a regular basis." In the conclusion of Book I, I noted that my sexual relations with black men did not lead to extensive participation in black social circles. Such integration is more difficult now, because I have a partner (as do many of those with whom I have sex). Moreover, I suspect that the black gay men who make sexual connections in the baths with white men are not particularly likely to participate in largely gay black circles. My friendship circle is far from being all-white and I rented the in-law apartment in our house to another black man who had the experience of going to see a series of apartments that were rented while he was en route. (Again, I knew, even if he didn't that he had not sounded black over the phone, but when he showed up…I didn't explain what had happened to him.) I do not accept any accusation of being interested in only the bodies (not the personalities and souls) of black men.

I can't say that I have no regrets about anything within these relationships. I regret that Lionel has kept our relationship confined to the walls of the Steamworks. I regret that Raju, Kevin, and Gerard dropped me—and that I only know why for Raju (he provided a fairly flattering rationale that he was falling in love with me).

I don't regret the effort (and time!) I devoted to G. I don't regret refusing to "give it up" to Rafael and to Kevin. If I entrust my vulnerable rear-entryway to someone, I do not want it to be on the first encounter (as it would have been with Rafael) or to someone whose interest in me is no deeper than however far his dick can burrow up my ass (my most hostile view of Kevin). I wish that I could better accommodate and give more pleasure to Lionel (and Raju), had been able to make G and the nameless man from chapter 7 cum. That is, I regret not being a more skilled cocksucker, but don't regret refusing access to meat deliveries in the rear. This last is a habit I do not want to revive.

I regret that I cannot make everyone I desire happy. I regret that not everyone whom I desire desires me and that I do not always please those who give me a try. These seem to me common facets of *la condition humaine*, not functions of being a white man who occasionally makes sexual connections with nonwhite men, or, specifically, black men. My understanding is limited, but this book has recorded what I experienced happening, how I observed and experienced myself and how I observed and experienced some black men with whom I was intimate (for varying lengths of time).

Some Notes on the Institutional Site of Connection

So many of the connections I have described herein occurred within gay bathhouses that, in closing, I feel I must say something about them—especially since they and other venerable venues for safe male-male sexual connection are under continuing attack by respectability-craving gay Republicans and by ostensibly liberal public health engineers (both gay and straight). Brush clearance of park areas where men meet and have sex with men is ongoing in San Francisco and elsewhere. The redevelopment of the Times Square area in Manhattan was part of a crusade against male-male sexual institutions in New York City, as *Policing Public Sex* and Samuel Delany (in *Times Square Red, Times Square Blue*) have discussed and cogently analyzed. Delany, an African American professor and writer, related some of his social and sexual encounters between the late-1950s and the late-1990s in Times Square theaters, providing a passionate and eloquent brief for the class-crossing contact that has traditionally occurred.

Delany insightfully notes that "if every sexual encounter involves bringing someone back to your house, the general sexual activity in a city becomes anxiety-filled, class-bound, and choosy." (p. 127) And, as he makes clear in his book, not everyone has a place to which sexual partners can be taken. Private space in which to have sex is a luxury in most of the world and for many American city-dwellers, too. There are many moral entrepreneurs (some of them gay and lesbian) eager to prescribe monogamy for others. (Often they consider themselves superior to the herd they seek to drive and in some instances don't practice what they preach.) AIDS has been used as a rationale to attempt to curb "promiscuous" homosexuality, remedicalizing homosexuality on the West Coast, recriminalizing it on the East Coast.

Those seeking to engineer male-male sexual institutions out of existence are unaware or indifferent to the needs of men for a physically safe place in which to have sex and of baths and other cruising grounds as homosocial—not just homosexual—sites. It is not just moralistic straight politicians like New York Mayor Rudy Giuliani, but also gay professionals like San Francisco Director of Public

Health Mitch Katz (who says he has never been a customer at a sex club or bath-house) who refuse to consider the multiple uses and meanings of institutions they seek to destroy, or to consider the lack of access to alternative sites for safe and private encounters (with showers) that many of those who go to gay bathhouses have.

Personally, I'd like the Ritch Street baths back. Without doubt, before anyone knew of AIDS, there was a lot of unprotected anal intercourse occurring there and in other gay bathhouses. But no one then knew what HIV was or how it was transmitted and how transmission of that virus could be blocked. In the many hundreds of hours I have spent across the bay in the Steamworks, I have not seen any unprotected anal intercourse. There has not been any in the rooms I have rented or visited, nor in the sex I have had in the semi-dark open spaces. At least 98 percent and probably more of the many thousands of sexual connection I have watched at the Steamworks have not involved anal sex at all. In the most seem-ingly feverish fucking that I watched, an ardent black top asked a spectator to hand him a condom before fucking an eager white bottom. Over the course of an hour, I saw him put on condoms three times. Similarly, when I have been suffi-ciently confident to mount proffered rear ends, most of the men have reached back to check that I was wearing a condom. (I always was.)

Businesses selling men access to other men are not utopias, and there is cer-tainly alienation within their walls, but, surely, no one believes these businesses are the cause of urban male alienation! Or that paternalistic governments forbid-ding such businesses decreases urban male alienation or enhances self-esteem among gay men. More than businesses, gay bathhouses are social institutions that have developed not only efficient provision of sexual contacts, but which have been sites for the origins of more enduring partnerships and friendships.[1] The need for the institution remains, badly understood as it is by those eagerly destroying it. The complicity by respectability-seeking gay men and lesbians in depriving men of their institutions is especially despicable. (For instance, before being indicted for several crimes including knowingly infecting a sexual partner with HIV, the openly gay San Francisco Health Commissioner Ron Hill expressed his embarrassment at gay bathhouses being discussed in that august body at the June 15, 1999 Health Commission meeting). Freedom of choice of

---

1. See work by Bérubé, Bolton, Delph, Dynes, Jones, Leap, Lee, O'Hara, Styles, Wein-berg & Williams cited in the bibliography. I am grateful to Stephen O. Murray, who called my attention to most of these publications, also urged me to include my reflec-tions on gay bathhouses in this book, and has promoted documentation of what he calls "erotic subjectivity," notably in the books by Khan and Ramos.

how to deploy our bodies and with whom should be as fundamental to gay men as it is to women since Roe v. Wade.

Bibliography

Baldwin, James. *Early Novels and Stories.* New York: Library of the Americas, 1998.

Beam, Joseph F. *In the Life.* Boston: Alyson, 1986.

Bérubé, Allan. "The history of gay bathhouses." *Coming Up!* 6,3 (1984): 15–19.

Bolton, Ralph, John Vincke, and Rudolf Mak. "Gay baths revisited: an empirical analysis." *GLQ* 1(1994):255–273.

Boykin, Keith. *One More River to Cross: Black & Gay in America.* New York: Doubleday, 1998)

Brandt, Eric. *Dangerous Liaisons: Blacks, Gays, and the Struggle for Equality.* New York: New Press.

Camus, Renaud. *Tricks.* New York: St. Martin's Press, 1981.

Constantine-Simms, Delroy. *The Greatest Taboo: Homosexuality in Black Communities.* Los Angeles: Alyson, 2001.

Corbin, Steven. *Fragments That Remain.* Boston: Alyson, 1993.

Corbin, Steven. *A Hundred Days From Now.* Boston: Alyson, 1994.

Dangerous Bedfellows. . *Policing Public Sex: Queer Politics and the Future of AIDS Activism.* Boston: South End Press, 1997.

Delany, Samuel R. *The Motion of Light in Water.* New York: Arbor, 1988.

Delany, Samuel R. "Aversion/perversion/diversion." In Monica Dorenkamp & Richard Henke, *Negotiating Lesbian & Gay Subject,* pp. 7–33. New York: Routledge, 1995.

Delany, Samuel R. *Times Square Red, Times Square Blue*. New York: New York University Press, 1999.

Delany, Samuel R. "Some queer notions about race." In Eric Brandt, *Dangerous Liaisons: Blacks, Gays, and the Struggle for Equality*, pp. 259–289. New York: New Press, 1999.

Delph, Edward William. *The Silent Community: Public Homosexual Encounters*. Beverly Hills: Sage, 1978.

D'Emilio, John. *Lost Prophet: The Life and Times of Bayard Rustin*. New York: Free Press, 2003.

Dixon, Melvin. *Vanishing Rooms*. New York: Plume, 1992.

Dowell, Coleman. *White on Black on White*, New York: Wiedenfeld and Nicolson, 1983.

Duplechan, Larry. *Eight Days a Week*. Boston: Alyson, 1985.

Duplechan, Larry. *Blackbird*. New York: St. Martin's Press, 1986.

Duplechan, Larry. *Tangled Up in Blue*. New York: St. Martin's Press, 1989.

Duplechan, Larry. *Captain Swing*. Boston: Alyson, 1993.

Dynes, Wayne R. "Bathhouses." *Encyclopedia of Homosexuality* 1(1990): 113–115.

Fisher, Gary. *Gary in Your Pocket*. Durham, NC: Duke University Press, 1996. (Posthumously edited by Eve Sedgwick.)

Gagnon, John, and William Simon. *Sexual Conduct*. Chicago: Aldine, 1973.

Grumley, Michael. *Life Drawing*. New York: Grove Weidenfeld. 1991.

Hakeswood, William G. *One of the Children: Gay Black Men in Harlem*. Berkeley: University of California Press, 1997.

Hall, Richard, *The Butterscotch Prince*. New York: Pyramid, 1975.

Harper, Phillip Brian. *Are We Not Men?: Masculine Anxiety and the Problem of African-American Identity*. New York: Oxford University Press, 1996.

Harper, Phillip Brian. *Queer Transexions of Race, Nation, and Gender* (=*Social Text*, 52–53). Durham, NC: Duke University Press, 1997.

Harper, Phillip Brian. *Private Affairs: Critical Ventures in the Culture of Social Relations*. New York: New York University Press, 1999

Hemphill, Essex. *Brother to Brother: New Writings by Black Gay Men*. Boston: Alyson, 1991.

Hemphill, Essex. *Ceremonies*. New York: Plume, 1992.

Henriksson, Benny. *Risk Factor Love: Homosexuality, Sexual Interaction and HIV Prevention*. Göteborg, Sweden: Göteborgs Universitet Institutionen för socialt arbete, 1995.

Hollinghurst, Alan. *The Swimming-Pool Library*. New York: Random House, 1988.

Humphreys, Laud. *Tearoom Trade*. Chicago: Aldine, 1975.

Jones, Bill T., with Peggy Gillespie. *Last Night on Earth*. New York: Pantheon Books, 1996.

Kamau. "A feeling within me" In *Boy-Wives and Female Husbands: Studies of African Homosexualities* by Stephen O. Murray & Will Roscoe, 41–65. New York: St. Martin's Press, 1998. (Interview conducted by Stephen O. Murray)

Kenan, Randall. *Let the Dead Bury Their Dead*. New York: Harcourt, Brace, Jovanovich, 1992..

Khan, Badruddin. *Sex, Longing, and Belonging: A Gay Muslim Life*. Bangkok: Bua Luang, 1997.

King, James L. *On the Down Low: Journeys into the Lives of "Straight" Black Men Who Sleep With Men*. New York: Broadway Books, 2004

Leap, William. *Public Sex, Gay Space*. New York: Columbia University Press, 1999.

Lee, John Alan. *Getting Sex*. Toronto: General, 1978.

Lockman, Paul T. Jr. "Ebony and ivory: the interracial gay male couple." *Lifestyles* 7(1984):44–55.

Loiacano, Darryl. K. "Gay identity issues among black Americans." *Journal of Counseling and Development* 68(1989):21–25.

Miller, Merle. *What Happened*. New York: Harper & Row, 1972.

Morrow, Bruce, and Charles H. Rowell. *Shade: An Anthology of Fiction by Gay Men of African Descent*. New York: Morrow, 1996.

Murray, Stephen O. *American Gay*. Chicago: University of Chicago Press, 1996.

Murray, Stephen O. "Subjectivities of some dark(-haired) objects of desire." *Journal of Homosexuality* 35, 1 (1998):114–133.

Murray, Stephen O. "Representations of desires in some recent Gay Asian-American writings." *Journal of Homosexuality* 45, 1 (2003):111–142

O'Hara, Scott. *Autopornography*. Binghamton, New York: Harrington Park Press, 1998..

Ramos, Ricardo. *Flipping*. Bangkok and Oakland, CA: Bua Luang, 1998.

Reid-Pharr, Robert F. *Black Gay Man*. New York: New York University Press, 2001

Scott, Darieck. *Traitor to the Race*. New York: Plume, 1996.

Scott, Darieck. "Why I need to be gang-banged to be turned on!" Pp. 38–58 in Michael Lowenthal (ed.) *Flesh and the Word 4: Gay Erotic Confessionals*. New York: Plume, 1997.

Smith, Charles Michael. *Fighting Words: Personal Essays by Black Gay Men*. New York: Avon.

Smith, Michael J. *Black Men/White Men: A Gay Anthology.* San Francisco: Gay Sunshine Press, 1983.

Styles, Joseph. "Insider/outsider: researching the gay baths." *Urban Life* 8(1979):135–52.

Underwood, Steven G. *Gay Men and Anal Eroticism: Tops, Bottoms, and Versatiles.* Binghamton, NY: Harrington Park Press, 2003.

Weinberg, Martin S., and Colin J. Williams. "Gay baths and the social organization of impersonal sex." *Social Problems* 23(1975):124–136.

0-595-30781-7

www.ingramcontent.com/pod-product-compliance
Lightning Source LLC
Chambersburg PA
CBHW061246280526
45784CB00002B/655